GIANTS OF
blues

Learn to play blues

guitar like the

all-time greats

from robert johnson

to eric clapton

Design: David Houghton

Music Engraving: Cambridge Notation
Music Transcription: Adrian Clark
CD Production: Adam Crute

Printed by: MPG Books

Published by: Sanctuary Publishing Limited, 82 Bishops Bridge Road, London W2 6BB

Copyright: Neville Marten, 1999

Photographs: courtesy *Guitarist* magazine

While the publishers have made every reasonable effort to trace the copyright owners for any or all of the photographs in this book, there may be some omissions of credits for which we apologise.

ISBN: 1 86074 211 4

GIANTS OF
blues

Learn to play blues

guitar like the

all-time greats

from robert johnson

to eric clapton

Neville Marten

introduction

What's so great about blues guitar then?

Well, one of the greatest things about blues guitar is that it's easy to get started. The blues scale is made up from a few simple notes which fall easily under the guitarist's fingers. On top of that, three easy chords are the basis for many, if not most blues songs. So, with a lead line or two under his belt and a basic knowledge of chords and keys, the beginner can soon start to sound convincing.

What's more, some of the greatest bluesmen of all time got by on incredibly limited techniques. But what they had, and what is fundamental to being a great blues guitarist, is expression. Provided you mean what you play and 'feel' it, you'll do okay.

And feel is perhaps the most important factor of all. You don't need the speed of Eric Clapton or Buddy Guy to wring buckets of expression from the guitar; the late, great Albert King would often play just four or five notes in a whole solo. And that's a mean blues guitarist if ever there was one.

Make that guitar talk

The guitar is a very vocal instrument; notes can be bent and slurred and generally created in a variety of different ways. Because of this, each player approaches the instrument differently, giving rise to the instant recognition of the greats. BB King, for instance, stands out for his choice of notes, his tone, his type of finger vibrato and his favoured positions on the guitar's neck. Clapton, whose note choices are never far away from those of BB, opts for a harder tone, attacking the strings with more vigour, playing faster and with more spite.

These are just two examples of why, with those few simple notes and basic chords, each player can create a palette of musical colour that provides instant personality. A musical fingerprint, if you like.

In this book I will try to get under the skin of some of the top blues players of all time, to see how they have used this particular musical form to create some of the most soulful, crying, sad, happy, exciting music on this planet.

In my monthly Blues Headlines column in *Guitarist* magazine, I have tackled the styles of a few of the world's great bluesmen. Here, using completely fresh solos and newly recorded backing tracks, I will examine many more; from the acoustic blues of Robert Johnson, right up to the scintillating style of Gary Moore. And many points in between.

Have fun... you could be the next Giant of Blues.

Neville Marten
January 1999

get playing
How to use the Giants Of Blues book and CD

The idea behind *Giants Of Blues* is simplicity itself. Each chapter focuses on one great player. I show you two 'signature' licks. These are licks which I feel are typical of this player and which you can learn by listening to the corresponding CD track. I then play a full twelve-bar solo which will incorporate these licks, plus other relevant phrases tying the whole thing together. Everything is written out in both traditional music notation and tablature, the system of fret and string numbers which shows you exactly where the fingers go and what they do when they get there.

As if that's not enough, there's a backing track for each chapter, so you can learn the licks, put the solo together and practise what you've learnt, at your own speed and in your own way. It's as if you could rehearse with the band at any time of the day or night.

And as your playing builds in confidence and skill, you'll soon be creating solos of your own. The potential to improve is enormous. It's all down to you, the time you have to spare and the dedication that you're prepared to give.

Sound advice

Now, you wouldn't expect me to leave it there, would you? Of course not. A budding bluesman needs to know a little about his forefathers, so each chapter gives a brief but interesting overview of each player's musical history.

Then, there's a whole section on the kinds of guitars that have featured in blues throughout the years, plus tips on which instrument might be right for a given style. There's even some guidance on the best tone for the occasion, with hints on amp settings and the effects – such as distortion or reverb – that you might like to add, to spice up your playing and make it sound just that little bit more authentic. I also suggest one album that sums up the style that each player is known for, to help you get through the mire and avoid wasted time and money.

All that's left to say is that I hope you enjoy reading and using *Giants Of Blues* as much as I enjoyed creating it for you. Good luck and, most especially, have fun!

My special thanks to...

Adam Crute for his backing tracks
Adrian Clark for his transcriptions
Mick Taylor for his invaluable help with the text
Eric Clapton it's all his fault
And every blues guitarist who's ever got up on stage and given it his best shot!

contents

cd track listing

Each chapter has four CD tracks: lick 1, lick 2, solo and jam track...

Track 1 Introduction
Track 2 Guitar tuning notes

Track 3 Robert Johnson – lick 1
Track 4 Robert Johnson – lick 2
Track 5 Robert Johnson – solo
Track 6 Robert Johnson – jam track

Track 7 T-Bone Walker – lick 1
Track 8 T-Bone Walker – lick 2
Track 9 T-Bone Walker – solo
Track 10 T-Bone Walker – jam track

Track 11 Elmore James – lick 1
Track 12 Elmore James – lick 2
Track 13 Elmore James – solo
Track 14 Elmore James – jam track

Track 15 John Lee Hooker – lick 1
Track 16 John Lee Hooker – lick 2
Track 17 John Lee Hooker – solo
Track 18 John Lee Hooker – jam track

Track 19 Muddy Waters – lick 1
Track 20 Muddy Waters – lick 2
Track 21 Muddy Waters – solo
Track 22 Muddy Waters – jam track

Track 23 BB King – lick 1
Track 24 BB King – lick 2
Track 25 BB King – solo
Track 26 BB King – jam track

Track 27 Albert King – lick 1
Track 28 Albert King – lick 2
Track 29 Albert King – solo
Track 30 Albert King – jam track

Track 31 Freddie King – lick 1
Track 32 Freddie King – lick 2
Track 33 Freddie King – solo
Track 34 Freddie King – jam track

Track 35 Buddy Guy – lick 1
Track 36 Buddy Guy – lick 2
Track 37 Buddy Guy – solo
Track 38 Buddy Guy – jam track

Track 39 Chuck Berry – lick 1
Track 40 Chuck Berry – lick 2
Track 41 Chuck Berry – solo
Track 42 Chuck Berry – jam track

Track 43 Eric Clapton – lick 1
Track 44 Eric Clapton – lick 2
Track 45 Eric Clapton – solo
Track 46 Eric Clapton – jam track

Track 47 Peter Green – lick 1
Track 48 Peter Green – lick 2
Track 49 Peter Green – solo
Track 50 Peter Green – jam track

Track 51 Jimi Hendrix – lick 1
Track 52 Jimi Hendrix – lick 2
Track 53 Jimi Hendrix – solo
Track 54 Jimi Hendrix – jam track

Track 55 Jimmy Page – lick 1
Track 56 Jimmy Page – lick 2
Track 57 Jimmy Page – solo
Track 58 Jimmy Page – jam track

Track 59 Paul Kossoff – lick 1
Track 60 Paul Kossoff – lick 2
Track 61 Paul Kossoff – solo
Track 62 Paul Kossoff – jam track

Track 63 Gary Moore – lick 1
Track 64 Gary Moore – lick 2
Track 65 Gary Moore – solo
Track 66 Gary Moore – jam track

Track 67 Stevie Ray Vaughan – lick 1
Track 68 Stevie Ray Vaughan – lick 2
Track 69 Stevie Ray Vaughan – solo
Track 70 Stevie Ray Vaughan – jam track

Track 71 Robert Cray – lick 1
Track 72 Robert Cray – lick 2
Track 73 Robert Cray – solo
Track 74 Robert Cray – jam track

Track 75 Walter Trout – lick 1
Track 76 Walter Trout – lick 2
Track 77 Walter Trout – solo
Track 78 Walter Trout – jam track

Track 79 Robben Ford – lick 1
Track 80 Robben Ford – lick 2
Track 81 Robben Ford – solo
Track 82 Robben Ford – jam track

general playing tips

As I've already said, to get started playing the blues you need a few chords and a few licks. Here are some of the favoured chords and scale patterns of blues guitarists; you can practise and get used to these in your own time.

You don't have to learn everything at once, but you can always refer back to these simple diagrams in the future.

Chords

Here's a small directory of the chord shapes that you're likely to encounter in blues music. I'll start with the easy ones and finish with some rather more sophisticated examples. Remember that chord shapes can be moved (transposed) up and down the fingerboard, into different keys.

OPEN CHORDS (NON MOVABLE)

E

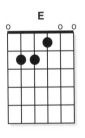

E7

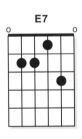

E7
(Easier)

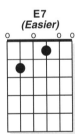

A

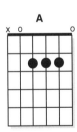

A7

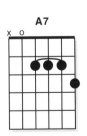

A7
(Easier)

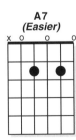

B7

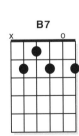

MOVABLE CHORDS:

Root on 6th string:

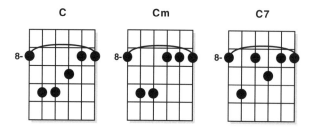

Root on 5th string:

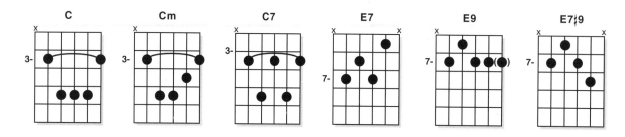

Fret numbers and top and bottom E-string note names

The fretboard (or fingerboard)

Before we start, here's a diagram of the guitar's fretboard, with all the frets numbered. Notice also that I've put a letter by each one. This is the name of the note on the top and bottom E strings at that particular fret and is immensely useful to learn. You see, each fret can give a huge and easy clue as to which key you're playing in, and therefore which fingering position to go for.

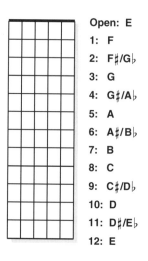

Open:	E
1:	F
2:	F♯/G♭
3:	G
4:	G♯/A♭
5:	A
6:	A♯/B♭
7:	B
8:	C
9:	C♯/D♭
10:	D
11:	D♯/E♭
12:	E

From the 12th fret, the pattern continues as from the open position

One of the most useful things you can do is commit this diagram to memory. And here's why...

The top and bottom strings are both E notes – high and low. As you play along these strings, the note changes by one semi-tone per fret: pluck either of these strings 'open' (without fretting) and it rings out with a note of E; play the next fret and it's F, and so on. Check the diagram below for the complete picture.

Coincidentally, a basic, E-shape barre chord played at any fret, has the same name as the E strings at that position. So, a barre chord played at fret five is a chord of A; at fret seven the same shape becomes B. Simple!

And it gets even better. The scales I'm about to show you are also rooted in the same way. So a minor pentatonic at fret five is A minor pentatonic; at fret seven the same scale shape becomes B minor pentatonic. Now isn't that fortunate!

True music teachers will probably rap my knuckles for making you think this way because, in absolute terms, 'positional' playing is not reckoned to be the best thing for your broader understanding. I'll just apologise and say that, if it's good enough for Gary Moore...

The next diagram has all the notes on all the frets on all the strings. This will take a little longer to learn, but it will give you a great advantage when working out licks and solos in tablature.

Fret numbers showing note names on all strings

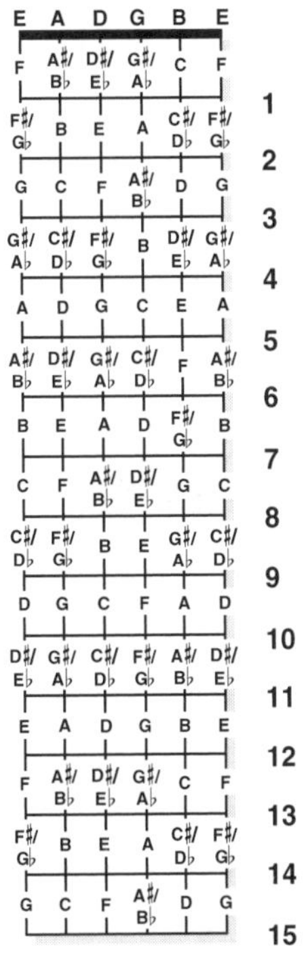

Fret	E	A	D	G	B	E
open	E	A	D	G	B	E
1	F	A#/Bb	D#/Eb	G#/Ab	C	F
2	F#/Gb	B	E	A	C#/Db	F#/Gb
3	G	C	F	A#/Bb	D	G
4	G#/Ab	C#/Db	F#/Gb	B	D#/Eb	G#/Ab
5	A	D	G	C	E	A
6	A#/Bb	D#/Eb	G#/Ab	C#/Db	F	A#/Bb
7	B	E	A	D	F#/Gb	B
8	C	F	A#/Bb	D#/Eb	G	C
9	C#/Db	F#/Gb	B	E	G#/Ab	C#/Db
10	D	G	C	F	A	D
11	D#/Eb	G#/Ab	C#/Db	F#/Gb	A#/Bb	D#/Eb
12	E	A	D	G	B	E
13	F	A#/Bb	D#/Eb	G#/Ab	C	F
14	F#/Gb	B	E	A	C#/Db	F#/Gb
15	G	C	F	A#/Bb	D	G

**Notice how the pattern of notes
from the 12th fret duplicates
the pattern from the open position**

Scales

Now, don't worry. Although the sheer mention of that word sends most guitarists scurrying for their security blanket (I always think of scale practice as musical square-bashing), you need to know very little of scales, modes and musical theory to be a good blues guitarist. Don't get me wrong; musical knowledge is a truly wonderful thing, and if you want to learn more, then there are many fine books available including David Mead's *Guitar Workout For The Interminably Busy* (see back page for more Sanctuary Techniques titles).

In *Giants Of Blues* you will find that many, if not most of the solos use the following four scales:

Minor pentatonic
Major pentatonic
Blues
Mixolydian

The pentatonics are so called because they use five notes (penta is Greek for five). Here they are on the guitar's fingerboard at fret five, and therefore in the key of A.

Minor pentatonic scale

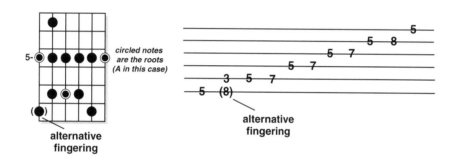

Notice that the 'home' fret, in this case fret five, is very easy to locate using this shape.

Major pentatonic scale

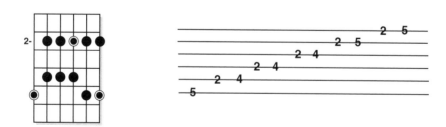

Notice here that the highest note of A (on the top E string) falls on the home fret.
These visual prompts are good to remember.

Blues scale

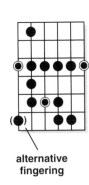

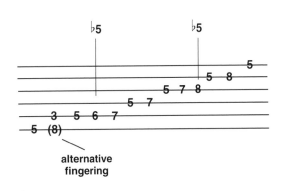

alternative
fingering

alternative
fingering

The blues scale is simply the minor pentatonic with one note added. This note is the flattened fifth of the major scale and gives a more exciting, 'tense' feel to the sound.

Mixolydian scale

(Partial fingering)

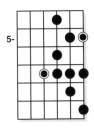

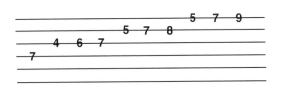

This scale is a favourite of more advanced blues players, because it has more 'interesting' notes in it. It's actually a normal major scale with the seventh note flattened by a semitone. Just sing 'do re me fa so la ti do' and flatten the 'ti' by a semitone. Easy or what?

Useful scale pattern positions

Most blues players play 'positionally'; that is, there are certain positions on the guitar's fretboard where clutches of notes fall under the fingers in a very useful way. Here is the most commonly used scale for blues – the minor pentatonic – in several different positions on the guitar neck.

(a)

(b)

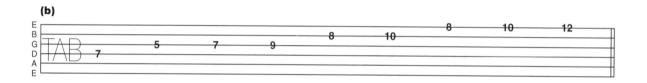

(c)

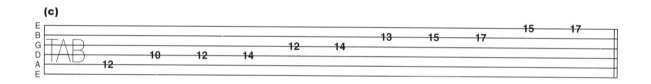

You will gain immensely from learning these positions. And since the other scale types relate quite closely to these minor pentatonic shapes, you'll soon find the relevant positions for those scale shapes too.

String bending

This topic could take up a whole book on its own. String bending is crucial to modern blues playing – I know I couldn't get on without it, and virtually every player in this book makes a feature of it.

It's possible to bend any string on the guitar. And you can bend them as far as the strength in your fingers will allow. But let's be sensible here; certain strings are bent all the time and others seldom bent at all.

Look at the diagram of the minor pentatonic scale opposite. I've shown the favourite strings for bending and the distances you can bend them by. Commonest bends are: semi-tone (one fret's distance); tone (two frets' distance); and minor third (three frets' distance). You can bend four and even five frets' distance (major third and fourth); Jimmy Page and Gary Moore sometimes use a four-fret bend, but a five-fretter is very rare in blues.

A minor pentatonic

Possible bends

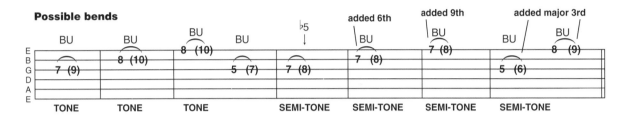

Extended position

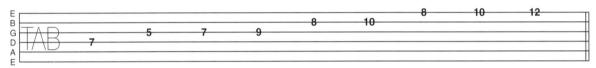

Possible bends

Hinting at the major pentatonic

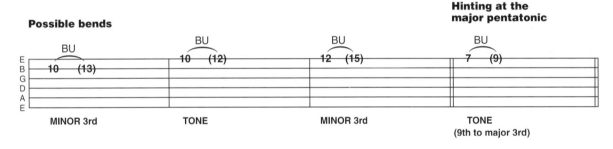

Fingers one, two and three are usually used for string bending in blues. When bending, try to 'support' the bending finger with an adjacent one. It's easier on the digits and allows more control over the note – especially if you're using finger vibrato. Most guitarists bend the string by 'pushing' it up, across the fingerboard, but others prefer to 'pull' it down. I often use both methods, so just do what comes most naturally.

Finger vibrato

There are many types of finger vibrato, and it's often this single element that sets one guitarist apart from another. Just think of Paul Kossoff's manic wobble and compare that to Robben Ford's total control of the string's movement.

Eric Clapton once said that vibrato was the most difficult guitar technique to master. To get yours sounding authentic, authoritative and natural

might take a while – especially at the top of a bent note.

Eric holds his hand away from the neck and literally wobbles it up and down, pulling and pushing the string and causing the note to oscillate in sympathy. BB King presses the string down and rotates his wrist back and forth (fret a string and then try to wind an imaginary, automatic wristwatch). I like to keep a firm hold of the guitar's neck, as it allows me greater control. I'm sure you'll discover your own vibrato soon enough.

What I would say is, don't copy the deliberate and very wide vibrato of rock and metal players; even Gary Moore, whose vibrato is among the most violent in this book, keeps it sounding 'bluesy'.

Over to you

And now it's your turn. You needn't go through these examples in any particular order, but in the long run you'll gain the most by examining as many as possible.

And while this book seems to be based on learning the guitar by ripping off the styles of others, there's absolutely nothing new or immoral in that. Most great musicians learn by listening to their heroes and taking on board not just their licks, but their musical inspiration as well. The many quotes that I've included from famous players should quell any pangs of plagiaristic guilt!

As Eric Clapton once told *Guitar Player* magazine: "Funnily enough, what I like about my playing is still the parts that I copied. If I'm building a solo I'll start with a Freddie King line, then go on to a BB King line and then do something to join them up. And that part will be me."

robert johnson
Down to the crossroads

BORN *c 1911, Mississippi USA.*

DIED *16 August 1938.*

Unfortunately best known for the alleged selling of his soul to the Devil down at 'the crossroads', Johnson was, however, one of the most powerful and influential bluesmen ever.

Like most blues artists of his generation, Johnson's style and technique were a distillation of those of his own heroes, notably Son House and Charley Patton, honed in seedy bars and barrel-houses wherever he could get a gig. Johnson's own creativity, vocal power and strident guitar work – sometimes bottleneck, sometimes not – added a dimension which would make him the template upon which other great bluesmen, including Howlin' Wolf, Muddy Waters and Elmore James, built their own careers.

While his recorded output may be limited – less than thirty tracks over a half-year period between 1936 and 1937 – this small body of work shows how advanced was his musical thinking and sophisticated his use of the guitar. True, it might seem crude by today's standards, but to really copy Johnson's style is a lifetime's work. It's often hard to see exactly how he made those sounds at all.

Although many of Johnson's lyrics focused on the mother's milk of early bluesmen – liquor, women, the road, the Devil etc – there were also deeper, more dramatic and emotional moods underlying his songs.

Best moments are perhaps 'Kind-Hearted Woman Blues', 'If I Had Possessions Over Judgement Day', 'Come On In My Kitchen' and, of course, 'Cross Road Blues'. The latter track was taken by Eric Clapton and transformed into 'Crossroads', featuring on the live disc of Cream's double album *Wheels Of Fire*.

To summarise Johnson's position in blues, it's probably no exaggeration to say that he was the most influential bluesman of all; his songs are still performed today and his legacy will survive as long as the blues itself.

He died in August 1938, poisoned by a jealous husband while performing near Greenwood, Mississippi. A sad but fitting end to the original blues giant.

Recommended listening
King Of The Delta (Mojo Workin').

In their own words
"I've run into a lot of players who thought it came from Jimmy Page or Jeff Beck or Buddy Guy or BB King. Well it comes from further back. And if you go back and listen to Robert Johnson and Blind Blake and Blind Willie Johnson and Blind Willie McTell, there's thousands of them that all have something that led to where it is now. The beauty of it is that you can take one of those things and make it *yours*."
Eric Clapton, speaking in *Guitarist,* June 1994.

Sound advice
This kind of blues comes from a long long time ago, before the advent of electric guitars and at a time when blues guitarists weren't the millionaires they are (at least some of them) today. So, you'll need an acoustic instrument and it doesn't really matter how good it is. Fit it with fairly heavy strings and, if you can bear the action a little on the high

biography

side, then all the better. That said, a lot of the old bluesers' guitars had rattling frets and very old strings – often broken and tied together again.

It's going to be difficult, if not impossible, to sound exactly like Johnson – and to be honest, I doubt there's anyone who really can – so the best thing is to try to catch the flavour. Lay back on it; don't worry too much about clarity, technique or timing; but try your very best to get that old time feel. It's as much as any of us can do. Johnson was a pure master.

Performance notes

I used a cheap, no-name acoustic for this. For the backing track, I tuned the guitar to E major (from the top down: E B G# E B E), but kept it in regular tuning for the 'solo'. Johnson would have done it all at once, probably tuned to E. If you want to get into this extraordinary player in a big way, you'll need to investigate open tunings and how to meld rhythm and lead lines together. For our purposes, I've split them up so you can play a few vintage-style licks over a backing track.

STYLE NOTES

● Licks generally built around underlying chords.

● Use fingerpicking for more authentic sound.

Robert Johnson Licks

Lick 1

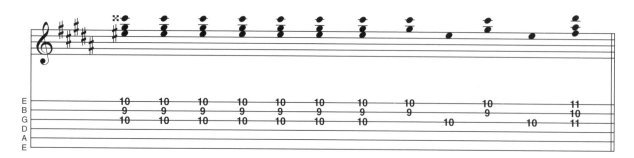

Lick 2

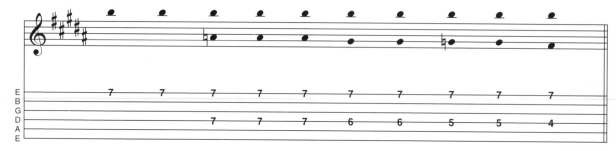

Robert Johnson Solo

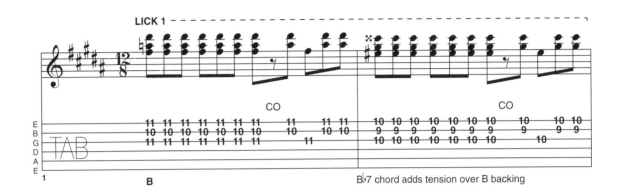

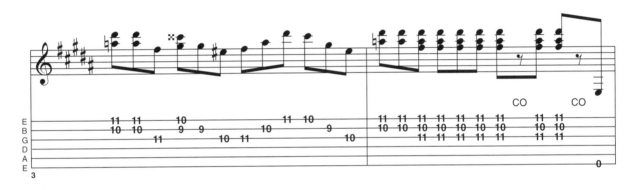

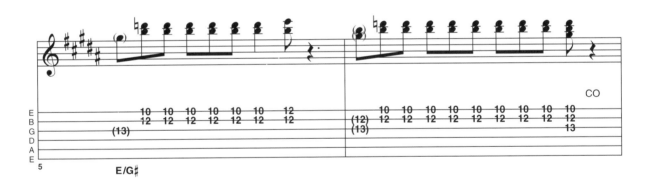

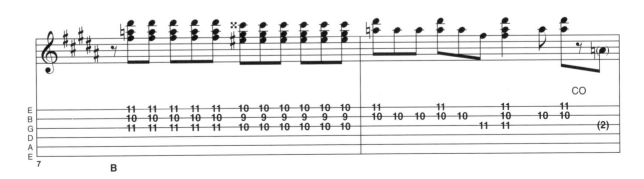

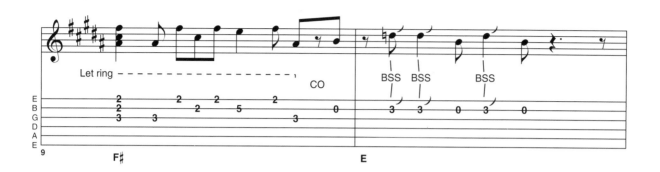

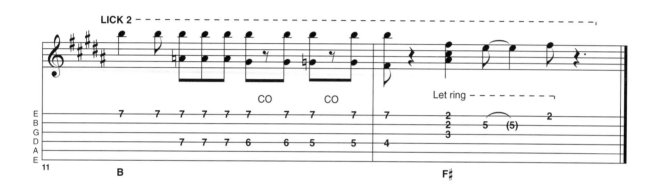

t-bone walker
Father of blues lead guitar

BORN 28 May 1910, Texas USA.

DIED 16 March 1975.

Just as Robert Johnson's influence as a singer, songwriter and general blues guitarist is paramount, so T-Bone Walker can be regarded as the man who defined the electric lead guitar style that forms the basis of blues playing today. And as blues lead forms the basis of most other soloing styles, the guitar owes a big debt to Mr Walker.

Raised in Dallas, Texas, T-Bone (from his middle name, Thibeault) was exposed to all the blues players of the day through his mother and stepfather, who invited visiting musicians to their home to perform.

Walker was already earning a living in his teens, playing guitar, singing and acting as sidemen to various performers of the day, when he visited Oklahoma City and met Chuck Richardson. Richardson also taught the great jazzman Charlie Christian to play single-note solos and in fact the two young men – who already knew each other – began lessons on the same day.

Walker's style and tone are so modern, preceding the likes of BB King by at least a decade, that it's almost odd listening to his recordings today. The jazz-inspired backings, with stride piano, old-fashioned drums and upright bass are the only real give-away.

Not only a stunning musician – he played good piano, too – Walker was also a great showman. He would often play the guitar behind his head, or while doing the splits – something both Chuck Berry and Jimi Hendrix would emulate decades later. You can also hear Walker in Berry's lead playing, so perhaps T-Bone was the father of rock'n'roll guitar too.

One of his greatest songs is 'Call It Stormy Monday', a blues club favourite, a true classic and one of the most recorded slow blues of all time.

Recommended listening
The Complete Capitol/Black & White Recordings (Capitol).

In their own words
"I think that the first thing I can remember was my mother singing the blues as she would sit alone at our place in Texas. I got to bend the notes like Mama did when I was small; I used to listen to her when I was supposed to be in bed. She'd give me the chills sometimes, so I aimed at getting hold of some of them notes. My stepfather was a guitar player too, and all his brothers and my mother would play for their own kicks. Like on Sundays, everybody'd get together in the house and have a little drink, and they would tune up their instruments and play to themselves. People used to come and stand around and listen."
T-Bone Walker, speaking to *Living Blues* 1972/73.

Sound advice
T-Bone was one of the very first electric guitarists, along with Les Paul and Charlie Christian. He was fortunate enough to play great guitars, his most well-known instrument being

biography

Gibson's fabulous ES250, a jazz-style archtop, one notch up from the ES150 that Christian used, and which is today known by his name.

Look for a warm tone, with little treble. It's unlikely that you'll own anything like the right guitar, but try using the neck pickup on any guitar, or the neck or middle setting on twin humbucker instruments. A small valve amp is favourite, but any amplifier with a little gain and the bass and middle controls turned up, will make a good stab at the T-Bone tone.

Effects? Not really; maybe the tiniest touch of reverb, to approximate a small jazz club, and perhaps a smidge of slapback echo to make you sound a little more spritely.

Performance notes

For the whole *Giants Of Blues* CD I used just two electric guitars: a Gibson Les Paul and a Fender Stratocaster. Everything went through a Marshall JMP-1 and straight into the desk. This shows how much variation your ears can bring to what might appear to be a limited repertoire of instruments. The T-Bone track features the Les Paul on the neck pickup.

Listen carefully to this track and you'll see how the T-Bone influence surfaces in the playing of other artists later on – BB King, Chuck Berry and Jimi Hendrix to name just three. Some influence, eh?

STYLE NOTES

- Use downstrokes for more authentic feel.

- Main scale: C minor pentatonic (C E♭, F G B♭, C) but with frequent addition of E (major 3rd) and A (sixth).

T-Bone Walker Licks

Lick 1

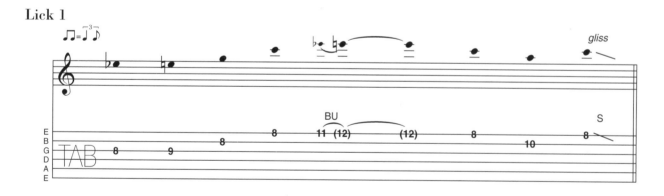

Lick 2

T-Bone Walker Solo

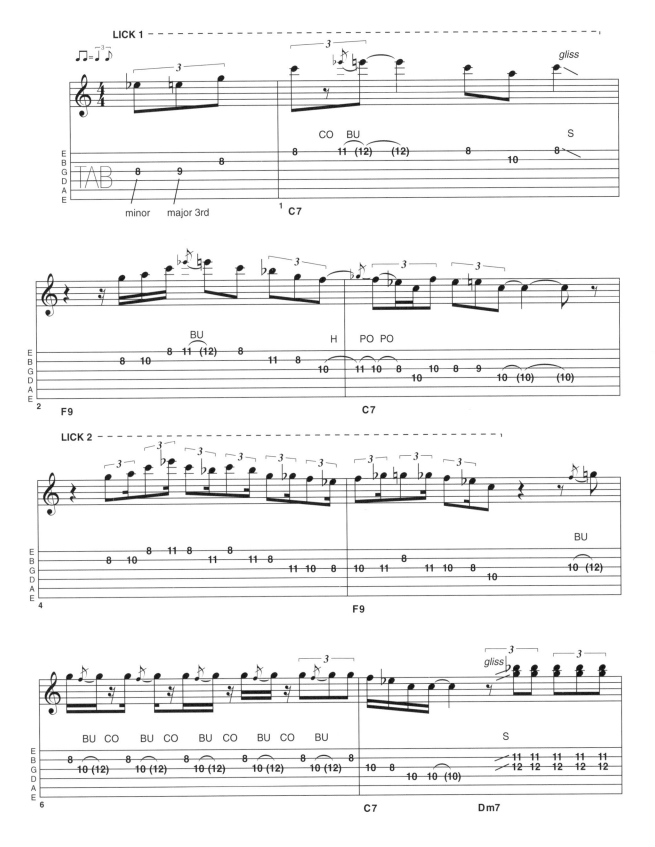

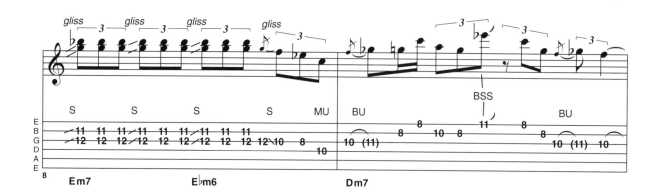

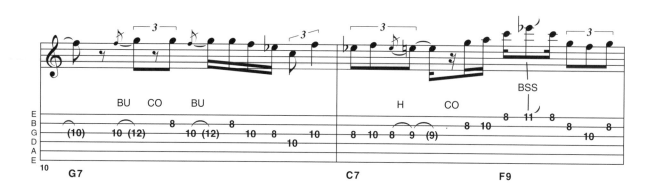

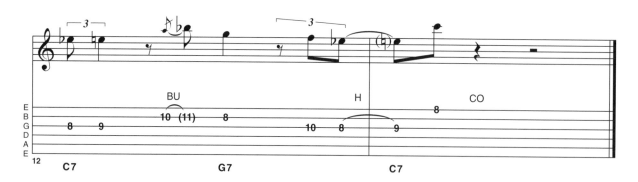

elmore james
Slippin' and a-slidin'

BORN *27 January 1918, Mississippi USA.*

DIED *23 May 1963.*

Think of Elmore James and one guitar phrase will inevitably shoot into the brain: diddly diddly diddly diddly deedum. Yes, it's that famous bottleneck intro to the Robert Johnson composition 'Dust My Broom', which James subsequently made his own. This intro became as much of an Elmore James trademark as Bo Diddley's equally famous 'Bo Diddley' rhythm.

That distinctive track was then followed up by others in the same vein, including 'Dust My Blues' and 'I Believe'. Elmore also befriended and worked as sideman to the great Sonny Boy Williamson, before moving to Chicago and forming a series of bands called, predictably, The Broomdusters.

James was a huge inspiration to the British bluesmen and fledgling R&B bands of the 1960s, who latched on to the guitarist's work just as he died; The Rolling Stones's Brian Jones, in particular, was a huge fan. But the two biggest carriers of the James banner were John Mayall, who recorded 'Dust My Blues' on his *Bluesbreakers With Eric Clapton* album and later penned the emotive 'Mr James'; and Jeremy Spencer of Fleetwood Mac, whose entire repertoire wreaked of the Elmore influence (when he wasn't doing Elvis impersonations, that is!). Fleetwood Mac also covered the James composition 'Shake Your Moneymaker', this time with Peter Green on vocals, while Jimi Hendrix would often feature Elmore's impassioned blues ballad 'Bleeding Heart' in his live act.

It's tragic to think that such a fine and influential performer would not live to see the impact that his music would have on those who followed him. Indeed, it would be interesting to see what Elmore would have made of all these middle class white Englishmen taking up his cause and spreading the word with such passion.

Recommended listening

Elmore James Box Set (Charly).

In their own words

"John Mayall used to play endless tapes, all different people; a hundred different people in one night. He had the whole of one wall done with a tape recorder and he used to play all these different people – BB King, JB Lenoir, Robert Johnson, Elmore James; millions of people."
Peter Green speaking in *Guitarist*, September 1993.

Sound advice

You can get away with using more or less any guitar on this style of bottleneck. Elmore would have used an acoustic for the majority of his life and Jeremy Spencer, Fleetwood Mac's honorary Elmore, played various guitars, from Strat to Les Paul. If you're playing electric, try the treble pickup first; if that's too sharp, then simply experiment until you find the sound that suits you best.

As with Robert Johnson, Elmore's style is so

biography

deeply entrenched, so peculiar to himself, that it's best to just follow the basic style – like Spencer did – to create as good an effect as possible.

Performance notes

The first thing to do is raise the action on your guitar and tune it to a chord of E (E B G# E B E); or D (D A F# D A D). To be in tune with me, you'll have to take the E option. The lower tuning is easier on the guitar, and is probably the best choice for acoustics.

James didn't use the kind of bottleneck vibrato that we often hear today, but you'll still need to gain control of that weird appendage (glass or brass are both fine) to sound convincing. I'm no slide player, but I prefer the tube on my ring

(third) finger, although others like the pinky (little finger). Experiment!

I used the Les Paul on the treble pickup and kept to very simple lead lines, basically just picking notes from the chords as each one changed.

STYLE NOTES

- Use of open tuning allows chords to be played with slide.
- Licks built around underlying chords.
- Major 3rd (G# in key of E) often played flat.

Elmore James Licks

Lick 1

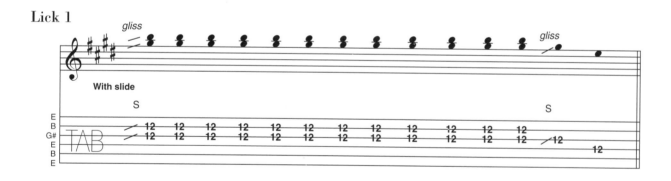

Lick 2

Elmore James Solo

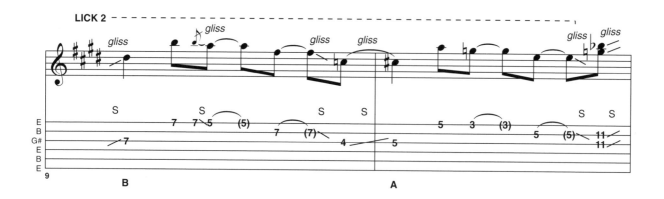

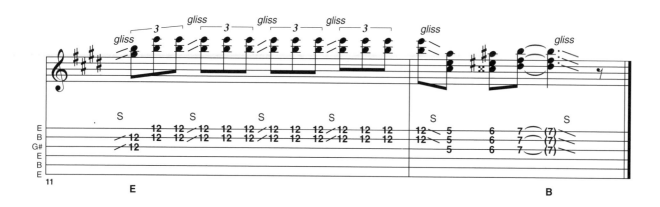

john lee hooker
Low down and dirty

BORN *22 August 1917, Mississippi USA.*

DIED –

John Lee Hooker is that rare thing among black American bluesmen; a legend in his own lifetime. He skipped home to Memphis at age fourteen, before arriving in Detroit in 1943. Here he made the first of many hundreds of recordings, often for different record companies under strange and sometimes transparent pseudonyms – John Lee Booker for the King label and John Lee Cooker on Chess, for example. 'Boogie Chillen' was his first commercial success in 1948; a song that has resurfaced on various compilations over the years.

Hooker's songs and guitar style are unique. Best known in the early days for his solo work – apparently his idiosyncratic timing made it difficult for bands to follow him – his thumping right foot was often his only accompaniment, save for an open-tuned electric guitar, on which he picked out fat chords and simple but effective lead lines. It was almost certainly Hooker who was parodied by Cheech and Chong in their hilarious skit 'Blind Melon Chitlin'.

Although successful from early on, John Lee's greatest triumphs have come late in life, assuring him a comfortable retirement and the adulation of fans and fellow musicians alike. Perhaps his finest recorded moments are on recent albums such as *The Healer* (1989), where artists like Bonnie Raitt and Carlos Santana added their considerable weight. On *Mr Lucky*, Hooker teamed up with one of his heroes, Van Morrison, as well as Ry Cooder and an array of other famous

devotees. The follow-up, *Chill Out*, saw both Santana and Morrison back in tow and even more success and acclaim for Hooker. Ad campaigns for beer, jeans and other cool commodities have used Hooker's music to great effect.

His last album was *Don't Look Back*, on which he cut new versions of old tracks such as 'Dimples', again with Van Morrison at his side and in the producer's chair. Long may John Lee Hooker reign as the grand old man of blues.

Recommended listening
The Healer (Silvertone).

In their own words
"There's just me and BB left now. I've never done anything different, just sung the blues. Now they call me a genius. But Eric Clapton, John Mayall and all those guys over in England made the blues a big thing. In the States, people didn't want to know, and it wasn't until the British guys made the American people listen that people like me, and Freddie King, Albert and BB King started to get a lot of people wanting to hear our music. It was our music originally, but it was those guys in England who made it big and then brought it back to the States."
John Lee Hooker, speaking in *Guitarist*, March 1997.

Sound advice
Hooker uses whatever guitar he fancies at the time, but is usually seen with Epiphone or Gibson semis. First port of call, tonally, is the

biography

middle selection on a twin humbucker guitar. That will normally do the trick, with only minor tweaking of the controls.

If you're a Strat player, I'd suggest the middle option again, but perhaps rolling off a touch of treble.

Effect-wise, we're talking minimal, but a touch of slapback delay will add a bit of bluesy authenticity, whether John Lee uses it or not. You see, what we're doing is going for the feel, rather than note-for-note copies; and if old blues sounds like it should have been slapbacked, then why not go for it.

Small combo amps are the thing, with not too much treble and hardly any gain at all; perhaps just enough to soften the edges a touch. Don't feel the need for stupendous accuracy, in either notes or timing; just go for the feel – get that foot thumping on the floor and you're halfway there.

Performance notes

This is a very simple track. If you're a learner, it will be a great place to start getting a little bit of dexterity in your fingers; and you can sound pretty authentic, quite quickly, too. If you're more advanced, go back and try to think 'minimal'; it never does anyone any harm.

The guitar was the Les Paul again, with both pickups on but the neck unit's volume turned down a touch.

STYLE NOTES

- Licks often built from small vocabulary of notes.
- Main scale used: E minor pentatonic (E G A B D E).
- Chord changes outlined by 'target notes'.

John Lee Hooker Licks

Lick 1

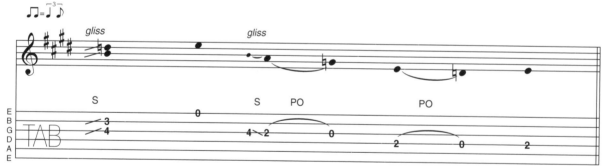

Lick 2

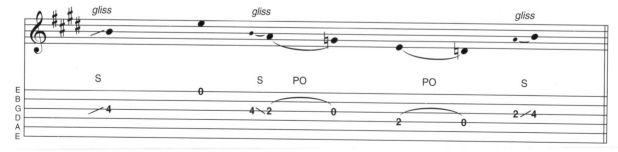

John Lee Hooker Solo

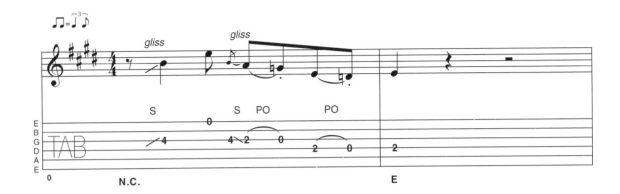

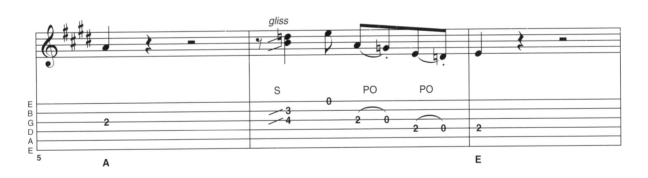

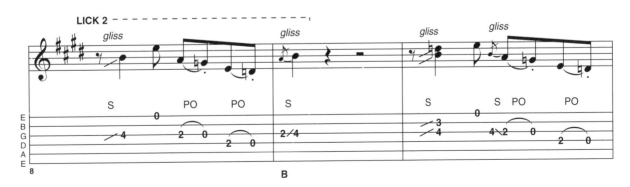

muddy waters
Influence for a new generation

BORN 4 April 1915, Mississippi USA.

DIED 30 April 1983.

McKinley Morganfield, as Muddy Waters was born, occupies a pivotal position in the history of the blues. Waters was a direct descendant of the early blues artists, such as Son House, Robert Johnson and Big Bill Broonzy. His move from Mississippi to Chicago at the age of twenty-eight, as an already accomplished musician, was to set the seal on a career which, while sometimes dubious as far as personal fortune was concerned, earned him unparalleled international respect and admiration.

When he toured Great Britain in the late 1950s his impact on the burgeoning British blues movement was remarkable. Influencing Alexis Korner and Cyril Davies, both regarded as fathers of British blues, as well as inspiring The Rolling Stones (who took their name from a Waters song) and many other subsequent blues heroes, Muddy was a perfect role model for the British blues boom of the 60s.

The list of seminal Waters songs is long and impressive, and includes such masterpieces as 'Rollin' And Tumblin'', 'Rolling Stone', 'Mannish Boy', 'Hoochie Coochie Man', 'I've Got My Mojo Working' and many, many more. Like the songs of John Lee Hooker, many of Waters' tracks have crossed over into the popular repertoire.

As was so often to be the case, although Muddy's reputation as a blues giant was secured, partly due to the patronage of British acts like the Stones and Led Zeppelin, his own success was patchy. And although he tried to borrow something back from his imitators – he covered Stones tracks and appeared on record with various well-known white guests – it never quite worked out. In 1983 he died of heart failure; a legend, but not the wealthy man his prolific and classy output might otherwise have suggested.

Recommended listening

King Of The Electric Blues (Mojo Workin').

In their own words

"We still have a lot to learn, but the people who were our teachers are now our friends. I got to meet Muddy Waters and play with him on stage. One of his guitarists had to return to Chicago so he said to me, 'Robert, do you think you can play that Muddy Waters style?' I said, 'Yeah, man!' So I got up on stage and played that thing!"

Robert Cray, speaking in *Guitarist*, January 1987.

Sound advice

Raw is a good word to describe the basic Waters touch. Dig in. Lay back. Don't worry too much about timing and tones, and forget effects completely. Instead, really do try to imagine what it must have been like to be a wandering black bluesman in the 30s and 40s. You'd have been very much a second class citizen, banned from white bars and restaurants and scorned by all whites, save those few who took the blues to their hearts and risked their own status by joining in.

biography

But in those seedy barrelhouses you were king; revered by men and idolised by women. This is the scene to set for yourself as you attempt to recreate the untechnical but brilliant work of a man like Muddy Waters.

Performance notes

With someone like Waters, whose style was based so much on untutored feel, it's as much the general vibe we have to capture as it is the tone of the great man's guitar. Muddy's most commonly used electric was a Fender Telecaster and he loved that rasping back pickup tone. He also tuned his guitar to a chord of E, but for our purposes I've kept to regular tuning.

This track was inspired by Muddy's early solo work, so whereas he would have played it all on one guitar, I've recorded a backing and added some Muddy-style licks over the top. He would have played a little less of both rhythm and lead than that.

But you know the most amazing thing about this aspect of the Waters style? Listen, and you can trace Hendrix's 'Voodoo Chile' right back to it!

STYLE NOTES

- Licks based on relatively small note vocabulary. (See also John Lee Hooker.)
- Main scale used: E minor pentatonic (E   G   A   B   D   E).
- Frequent bends to ♭5 (B♭).

Muddy Waters Licks

Lick 1

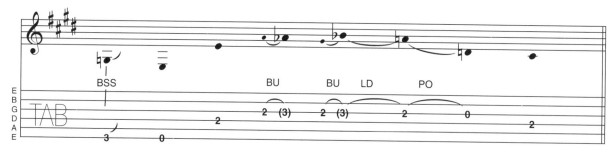

Lick 2

Muddy Waters Solo

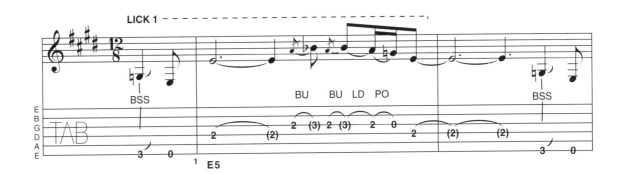

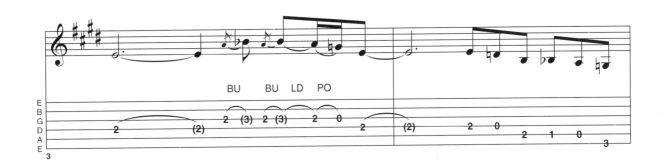

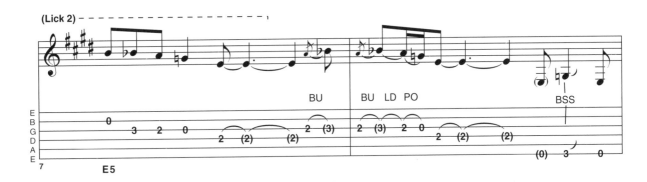

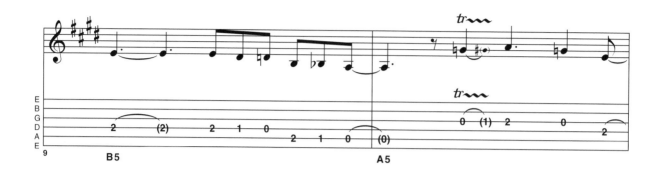

bb king
Right royal genius

BORN *16 September 1915, Mississippi USA.*

DIED –

B B King is a star. And from the very start of his career that's what he's always wanted to be. Almost unbelievably, he didn't begin playing until age eighteen. That he managed along the way to evolve a vocal and guitar style that would set him apart – and some would say a good deal above – his contemporaries, was just good fortune. It has also enabled him to stay abreast of changing musical whims and remain one of the world's hardest working guitarists.

His whole life is the stuff of legend, from his BB moniker, gained as a radio DJ in Memphis – he was known as Beale Street Blues Boy – to the incredible story of his guitar: Lucille. During a mid-winter gig at Twist, Arkansas, a burning oil drum was overturned in the middle of the dance floor; the result of a massive brawl over a girl. Two men died in the ensuing blaze and King – who almost lost his own life saving his guitar – named the instrument after the girl. Lucille was born.

Like many other black blues artists, King's leap in fame came from the patronage of white, often British, musicians who cited him as an influence. Eric Clapton happily attests to his copying of King's licks and John Lennon was quoted as saying that he longed to play guitar like BB. In trying to emulate the bottleneck style of his cousin, Bukka White, it is said that BB invented the finger vibrato so important to blues players today.

King is always pragmatic, respectful and thankful to the artists who have supported him. And although some may say that he now panders to a middle class white audience, the truth is that BB is blues' best possible ambassador. Ironically, he is now turning music fans on to other blues artists, just as Clapton, Green and company did for him over thirty years ago.

Recommended listening

Live At The Regal (MCA).

In their own words

"I've always tried hard to let people see that blues musicians can be well prepared, sober, and put on an entertaining show. I didn't finish high school, and the more popular I get, the more I see the need for the education I could have got, if only I'd worked a little harder at it. I'm constantly on my toes thinking, 'What can I do to make up for my lack of education?' And that's one reason I would never go unprepared for anything, no matter what it is, because I'm too dumb in other ways. Nowadays, anything I know that I can have better, or make better, I want better."

BB King, speaking in *Guitarist*, March 1992.

Sound advice

The aim is to get something which combines overall mellowness with a bit of cut, so not much middle on the amp but boost the bass and treble a touch. Again, BB's sound often contains a bit of drive, although never enough to make it sound distorted; it's that classic blues thing of finding the amp's 'sweet spot' and this is always easier on small combos, with a fairly low power rating. A touch of reverb will help it sound convincing.

biography

BB's tone has changed a lot over the years. In the early days it was quite biting and raunchy – the product of small valve amps not handling the guitar's output so well. Since the advent of the Gibson ES series, back in 1958, King has favoured these guitars due to their combination of cut and warmth. His signature 'Lucille' guitar today is a customised ES355 and BB will either opt for a both-pickups-on sound, neck pickup on its own, or occasionally one of the out-of-phase sounds available.

Performance notes

I used the Les Paul with both pickups on, and a tiny touch of drive on the Marshall preamp. It's a bit fat and a bit cutting.

It always feels strange to me, repeating licks as obviously as BB tends to do, but when he does it, nothing could seem more natural, or musical. What BB does is to make subtle changes to similar licks; changing an inflection here and there, rather than feeling the need to show off his chops – which he could if he wanted to. Remember that this is not a technique competition, and that those artists highlighted in this book whose technique is the least dazzling – at least as far as the number of notes played – are among the most revered.

Finally, listen to the BB, Albert and Freddie King-style tracks on this CD and then try to list the number of modern blues players whose style owes much, if not most, of its existence to these wonderful musicians.

STYLE NOTES

- Scales used: combination of G major pentatonic (G A B D E G) and G minor pentatonic (G B♭ C D F G).
- Use downstrokes only.
- Fast vibrato (BB shakes his whole hand, pivoting from the fingertip).
- Frequent use of scale position based around root note on B string.

BB King Licks

Lick 1

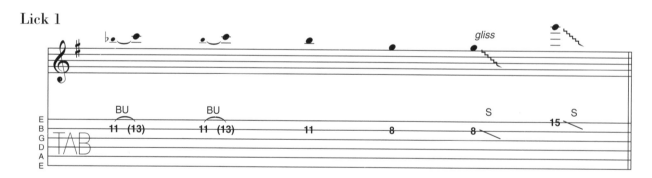

Lick 2

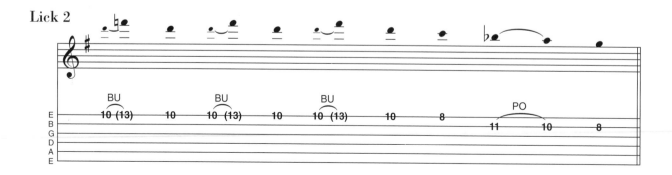

BB King Solo

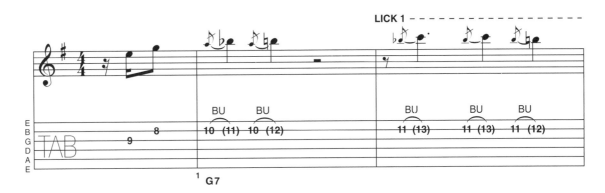

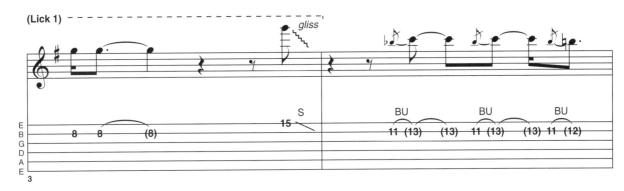

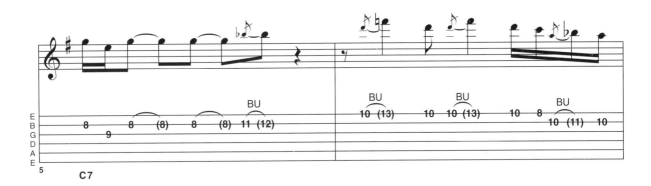

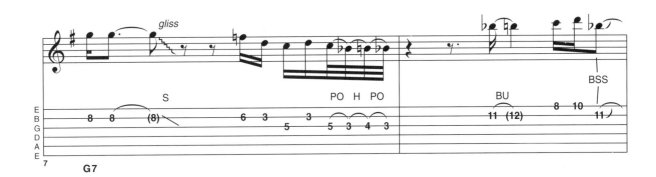

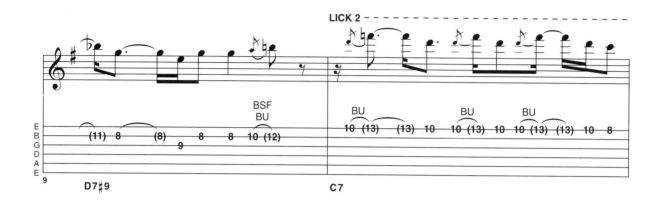

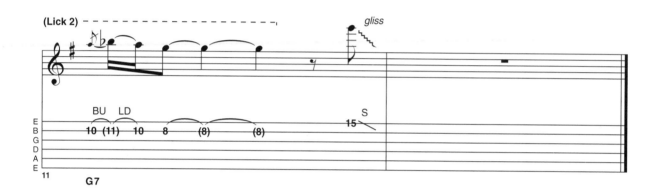

albert king
Heart and soul

BORN *Born c 1923, Mississippi USA.*

DIED *20 December 1992.*

One of the best loved of the Mississippi guitar playing singers, Albert King did not begin full-time performing until he was almost thirty. Recognised instantly by his left-handed Gibson Flying V, which he named Lucy, and a playing style so sparse as to defy belief, King was nevertheless a true blues master.

He loved jazzy, big band arrangements, where his guitar would act more as musical punctuation than as an outright solo instrument. This King was funky before funky existed!

'Born Under A Bad Sign', 'Oh Pretty Woman' and 'The Hunter' were King songs famously recorded by aspiring young fans of their mentor (Cream, Free, John Mayall and Gary Moore among them).

Unlike his more famous hometown namesake (it's been said that BB and Albert were distant cousins, both hailing from Indianola), Albert's career remained only sporadically successful. In the 1960s he teamed up with Booker T And The MGs to record some classic tracks, including those previously mentioned, as well as 'Cold Feet', which showed his lazy guitar and gruff, humorous vocals to superb effect.

Surprisingly, perhaps, this understated technique, which often concentrates on no more than four or five notes in a whole solo, was the inspiration for such dextrous fretboard dazzlers as Gary Moore and Stevie Ray Vaughan; listen to Vaughan's 'Texas Flood' for a perfect King take-off.

Gary Moore took Albert under his wing in 1990 (or was it the other way around?), when he invited him to record and tour after Gary's million-selling albums *Still Got The Blues* and *After Hours*. Sadly, in 1992, just when things were going right for Albert, he passed away.

Recommended listening

Best Of Albert King: I'll Play The Blues For You (London).

In their own words

"The last thing I want anybody to think is that I was trying to blow Albert King off stage. I could never, in a million years, blow him off as a blues player. You know, if we hadn't had him, we wouldn't have anybody that we know. Forget Clapton, forget Hendrix, people like me, Stevie Ray Vaughan; this whole generation. It's just ridiculous what he did with three or four notes. The guy's a genius at blues guitar. We spent three days in the studio and it was just great to be around the guy."
Gary Moore, speaking in *Guitarist*, March 1992.

Sound advice

Like BB King, Albert's tone has changed over the years. He has often tried to use more distortion, especially on his more riffy numbers, and his solid-bodied Gibson Flying V, with its powerful humbucking pickups, will have revelled in such tones.

Use just enough drive to help the notes carry, whilst retaining the inherent tone of the guitar; if you can hear the fuzz over the wood and the pickups, then you've gone too far.

TRACKS 27-30

biography

Performance notes

Albert's style was so laid back it wasn't true, with a big vibrato – almost pushing the guitar out of tune at times – and a minimal selection of notes. His left-handedness may well have played a part in his powerful vibrato, so you'll have to concentrate just that little bit harder on that aspect of his style. Add to that a very laid-back, almost behind-the-beat feel, and this King's sound, although based around the fewest notes of almost any blues giant, is a pretty tricky one to emulate. If you can't get the sound exactly right, go for the feel; it'll serve you better every time!

My guitar choice on this track was the Gibson Les Paul, with both pickups on and the treble turned full up on both controls.

STYLE NOTES

- Main scale: G minor pentatonic (G B♭ C D F G).

- Addition of major 3rd (B) despite minor key.

- For a more authentic sound, try plucking with your thumb.

TUNING: CBEF#BE

PLAYS MOST LICKS:

Albert King Licks

Lick 1

Lick 2

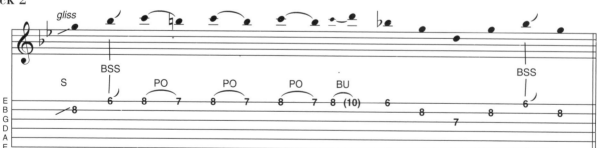

Albert King Solo

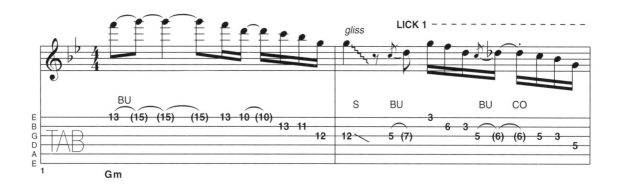

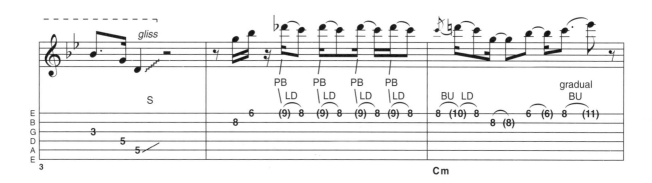

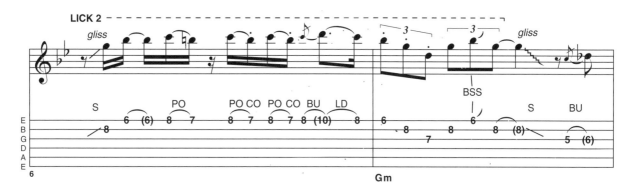

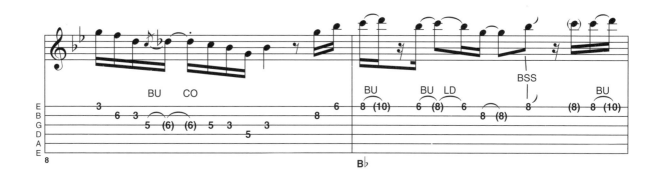

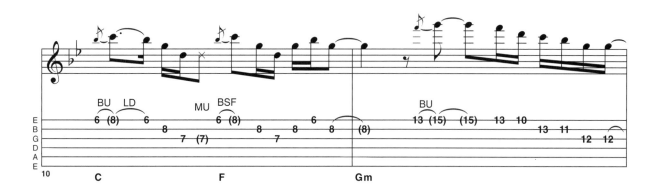

freddie king
King of the guitar instrumentals

> **BORN** *30 September 1934, Texas USA.*
>
> **DIED** *28 December 1976.*

Eric Clapton's 'Hideaway' and 'Steppin' Out', Peter Green's 'The Stumble' and Mick Taylor's 'Drivin' Sideways' have a dark secret in common; they're all Freddie King instrumentals. These compositions were perfect vehicles for other instrumentalists to cut their teeth, or display their new-found prowess.

King's ability and showmanship as a guitarist were evident early on, when he developed a fiery style that drew admiration wherever he played. Built on the influence of players like T-Bone Walker, Freddie's flashy style led to his joining several prominent bands when he moved to Chicago at the end of the 1940s. Here he also came into contact with other great blues players. Particular heroes were Otis Rush and the great Magic Sam. His earliest recordings as Freddie King came in 1960 and included the classic 'Hideaway'.

Although perhaps best known for those great instrumentals, which were definitely his trademark when touring with his own bands, Freddie was also a consummate blues ballad writer. These included the emotive 'I'm Tore Down' and 'Have You Ever Loved A Woman', both of which have been successfully adopted by Eric Clapton.

The quality of his recordings over the years has been patchy, to say the least, and it has been said that other artists have made a better job of his songs than Freddie himself. Live, though, it was a different matter, and towards the end of his life Freddie joined Eric Clapton, among others, on stage and on record. Freddie loved a good guitar battle and would enjoy trading licks with other players. Rarely would he come off the worst in such encounters!

Sadly, Freddie died in 1976, but his songs and great guitar instrumentals live on, in every blues bar, in every town in the western world.

Recommended listening
Hideaway (Blues Encore).

In their own words
"I was interested in the white rock'n'rollers until I heard Freddie King. Then I was over the moon; I knew that was where I belonged – finally. That was serious, proper guitar playing and I haven't changed my mind ever since. I still listen to it in my car, when I'm at home and I get the same boost that I did then. For some reason it did something to me. I spent all of my mid to late teens and early twenties studying the music; studying the geography of it, the chronology of it. I was learning it as well and trying to figure out how I could apply it to my life."
Eric Clapton, speaking in *Guitarist*, June 1994.

Sound advice
The problem we have with Freddie's sound is that we're probably more used to the tones of Eric Clapton and Peter Green on covers of 'Hideaway' and 'The Stumble'. But Freddie's tone wasn't so far away from that; he loved to drive his amps hard and those late 50s, early 1960s recordings were often more overdriven than anything previously heard. No wonder it

biography

turned Clapton and Green on so much.

Freddie generally played Gibson semis, such as the stereo ES345, and would often try all the positions on the six-way Varitone switch, including out-of-phase options. This was a 'guitar straight into the amp man' so little in the way of effects will be needed; a touch of smoothing reverb, perhaps.

Performance notes

Freddie King adopted the basic fingering template laid down by T-Bone Walker, but played it faster and more fierily. He represents the perfect stepping stone between Walker and Eric Clapton: there's an almost seamless join if you listen carefully; they could have been grandfather, father and son, musically speaking.

When you play this piece, try to imagine how

confident Freddie must have been back in Chicago, as the guitarist on the top of the pile, musically and technically speaking. If you can get some of that 'flash' into your playing, all the better. While you're at it, pretend you're in a lick-swapping battle with Eric Clapton, at a dingy club in the Windy City!

STYLE NOTES

- Bright, melodic feel.
- Main scale used: E minor pentatonic (E G A B D E).
- Frequent addition of notes from E major pentatonic (E F# G# B C# E).

Freddie King Licks

Lick 1

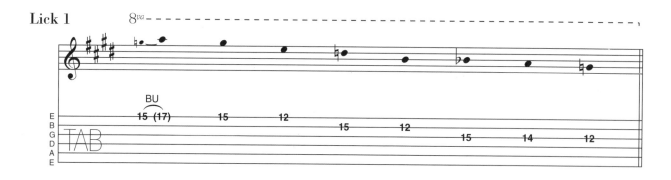

Lick 2

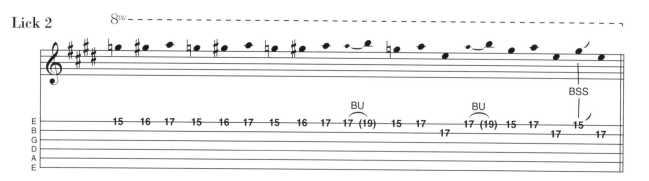

Freddie King Solo

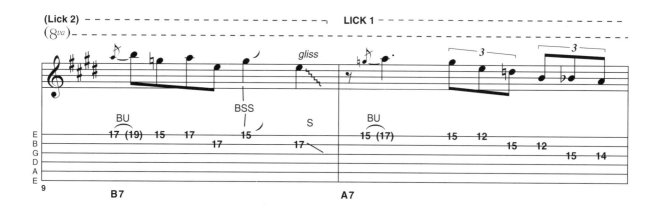

buddy guy
Blues fireworks

BORN *30 July 1936, Louisiana USA.*

DIED –

With his polka-dot shirt and matching guitar, Buddy Guy cuts an impressive figure as he struts the stage.

Although best known for his edgy, fast-fingered lead style, Buddy is equally at home singing solo with an acoustic guitar. It's this side of Guy's persona that reveals a bluesman of yore. Born not long after Freddie King and yet somehow endowed with the powers of a much younger man, Guy could be a contemporary of Walter Trout, rather than a man approaching twenty years his senior.

The influential Willie Dixon introduced Guy to Chess records and, as guitarist in the Chess house band, he played on the records of such legends as Muddy Waters and Howlin' Wolf. His early solo albums on the Vanguard label showcased an excellent musician at the height of his youthful powers.

Although continuing to record throughout the 1970s and 80s, these decades were anathema to the blues and Guy's real return to popularity had to wait until 1990, when he guested at Eric Clapton's blues night at the Royal Albert Hall and the following year, with the help of Clapton, Mark Knopfler and Jeff Beck, recorded the excellent *Damn Right I Got The Blues*. Other good albums followed and in 1995 Buddy released the excellent live record *Live At The Checkboard Lounge*.

Guy is a strident performer and fine musician, whose stage presence commands considerable respect. Yet, the night I visited his Chicago blues club in 1991 – when his career was at its illustrious peak – guess who was taking the money on the door. That's it: the quietly charming Mr Buddy Guy.

Recommended listening

Damn Right I Got The Blues (Silvertone).

In their own words

"My dad found a guy who had a guitar with a couple of strings on it. I got hold of that for a couple of bucks. But there was nobody I could look up to and say, 'One day I'll be like that, up on that stage.' Finally my dad got one of those Victrolas and I was beginning to hear records from T-Bone Walker, BB King, John Lee Hooker, Muddy Waters, Little Walter and Howlin' Wolf. I said, 'Jesus Christ, I'm glad I kept fooling with the guitar. Man, just listen to *that*!'"
Buddy Guy, speaking in *Guitarist*, January 1989.

Sound advice

Buddy's a Fender Stratocaster player these days and likes an edge to his sound, to give the aggression that comes across so well in his style.

You'll often hear him using the treble pickup on its own, or position two, with the neck and middle pickups selected together. For more subtle stuff he'll opt for the front pickup for that 'flutey' tone which Hendrix liked so much – Jimi was a big Guy fan.

Fender amps, with quite a bit of edge and overdrive added, provide the body to the Buddy tone, but any decent amplifier, with all the tone controls set quite high, should provide the right

biography

sonic landscape to practise those fast lines. To me, Buddy sounds like one of those players who seem 'cleaner' than their amp settings imply.

Effects-wise, a little reverb will generally suffice, but you could add a touch of slapback delay to help create the live feel so important to blues.

Performance notes

Although he uses similar patterns to many of the guitarists featured in this book, Buddy Guy will often play a note straight, where others would have bent it; especially at the end of a run. His vibrato lacks the utter control of a Clapton or Hendrix, but this just lends an extra personality trait to Buddy's playing. Just as T-Bone is still heard in the styles of BB King and Eric Clapton, so you can hear a strong Guy influence in artists such as Robert Cray and Walter Trout. It's this

identifiable musical lineage that makes blues guitar so fascinating, and which I hope *Giants Of Blues* is demonstrating to you.

I used the Fender Stratocaster with bridge and middle pickups selected, and a light overdrive added to the Marshall preamp.

STYLE NOTES

- Main scale used: B♭ minor pentatonic (B♭, D♭, E♭, F A♭, B♭).

- Frequent addition of ♭5 'blue note' (E in this particular key, often written 'F♭').

- Phrases are rhythmically very freeform.

Buddy Guy Licks

Lick 1

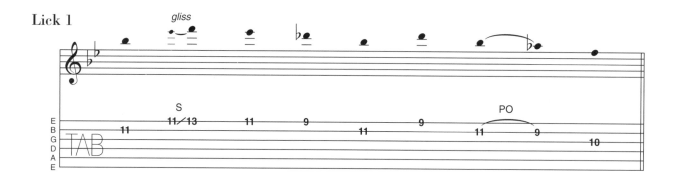

Lick 2

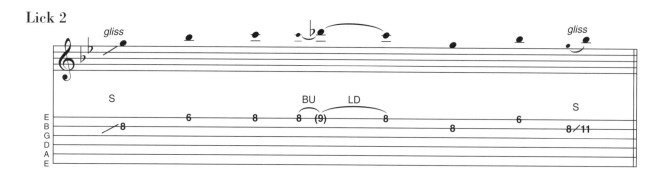

Buddy Guy Solo

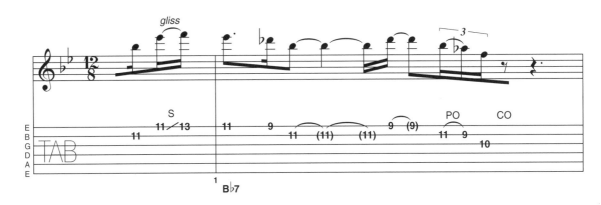

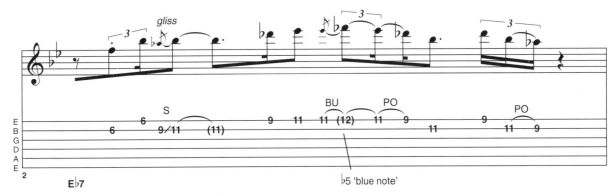

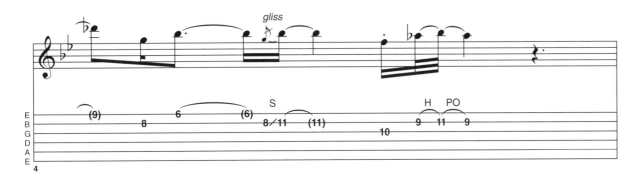

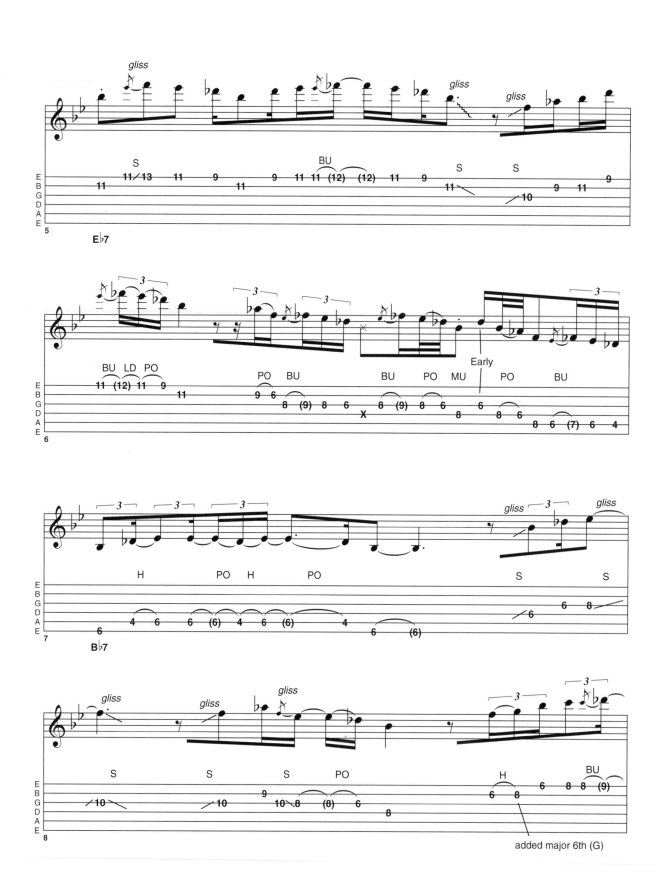

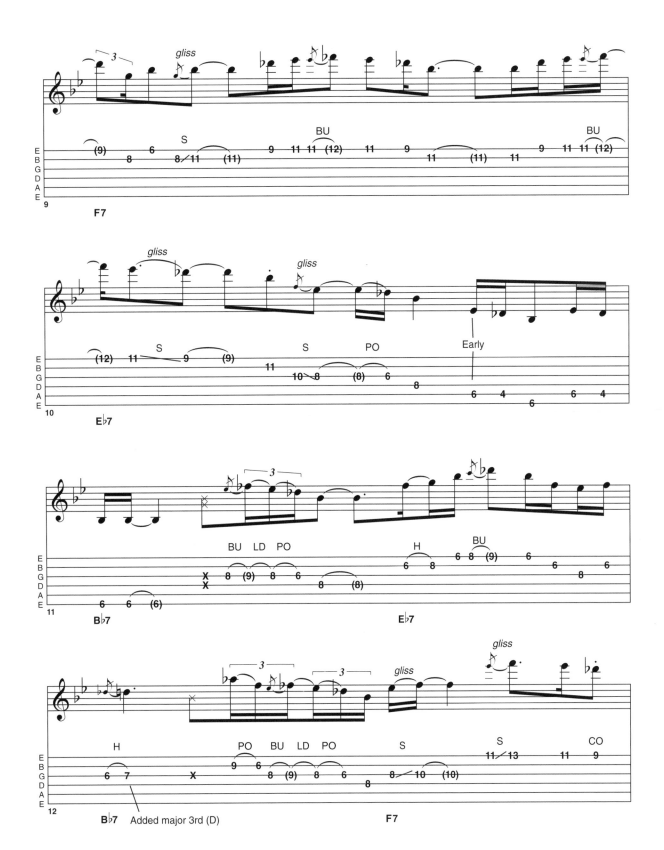

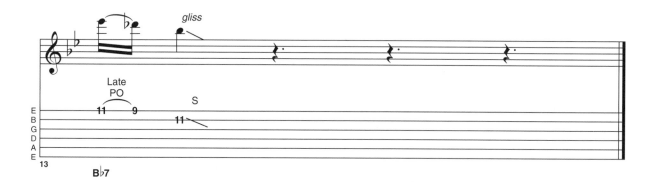

chuck berry
From blues to rock

BORN *18 October 1926, Missouri USA.*

DIED –

Although Charles 'Chuck' Berry is hardly regarded as a bluesman, the relationship between rock'n'roll and blues is so close as to make the question academic. What's more, Chuck's admitted affection for the great T-Bone Walker was such that the roots of his music stem from true blues. He also confesses to have plundered the styles of Charlie Christian and Elmore James. And why not? That's precisely what we're doing here. And what self-respecting blues band hasn't ended a stomping evening with 'Johnny B Goode'?

Berry's claims of attempted escape from his crib, while listening to his parents' gospel singing in an adjacent room, must surely be believed. That he was also tapping his feet in time, aged just a few months, is evident from the music he invented some thirty years later. Chuck's back-beat rhythm really does have your soul singin' the blues.

So, whether we accept this early rock music as blues or not, the subjects covered in Berry's imaginative lyrics are exactly those of the blues: women, automobiles, trouble and the general stresses of life. That those three chords echo exactly those of blues is just another indication of rock'n'roll's kinship.

Berry's life has been one of incredible ups and downs. Spells in jail and periods of financial hardship are interspersed with spectacular success – Chuck reckons a major problem hits him about every fifteen years.

Stories abound of the artist turning up minutes before showtime, demanding cash up front and expecting the pick-up band to know all his songs with no prior rehearsal. As Bruce Springsteen explained when it happened to him as a twenty-three-year-old: "I said, 'What songs are we going to do?' He said, 'Well, we're going to do some Chuck Berry songs.' That's all he said."

Recommended listening
Chess Masters (Stylus Music).

In their own words
"I grew up on Little Richard and Chuck Berry. Good rock'n'roll is hard to come by. I never really plugged into Elvis; not even The Beatles, except when they played a rock'n'roll tune and then they were really cooking. There's one thing that stands out on guitar for me, and that's Chuck Berry's 'Johnny B Goode'. You hear that, and you immediately know what it is. And if you can come up with something like that, great. As long as it's different but still you; that's the challenge. You can always find new ways of looking at things. Hey, you might even get a 'Johnny B Goode'!"
Angus Young, speaking in *Guitarist*, March 1998.

Sound advice
Yet another Gibson semi fan, Chuck has been seen with ES355s, ES350s, ES335s, ES330s and probably every other version of this most famous guitar line. Chuck will often turn up to a gig and play through whatever amp is there on the night – usually a Fender Twin Reverb of some sort – so his live sound will vary according to prevailing conditions.

biography

On his recorded classics, it would seem as though the guitar is set in the middle position (both pickups on) to provide that mix of bass and cut which so symbolises the tones of the three Kings. Certain things were undoubtedly bridge pickup only, but the safest bet is that middle setting.

Either no effects at all or the mildest hint of reverb and slapback will provide the most authentic Chuck Berry tone.

Performance notes

That famous 'Johnny B Goode' intro owes so much to T-Bone Walker it's not true. Listen to the Walker and Berry tracks back to back and see for yourself. There's very little in the way of vibrato in Chuck's playing, but use plenty of double stops (more than one string at a time), and don't be too worried about fingering accuracy; Chuck never seemed to and it added to that great, rebellious feel.

Don't forget, too, that players like Keith Richards of The Rolling Stones and Angus Young of AC/DC also have their own versions of the Berry sound, so check these out too, just in case your favourite falls somewhere in the middle. It was Les Paul again here, on that ubiquitous 'both pickups on' setting and just the smallest hint of drive on the amp.

STYLE NOTES

- Frequent use of double stops.
- Licks often built around underlying chords.

Chuck Berry Licks

Lick 1

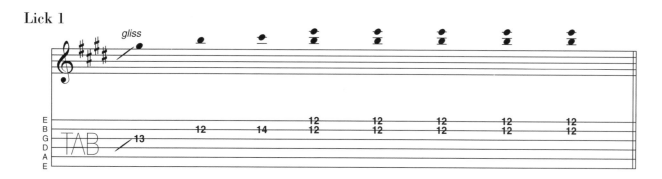

Lick 2

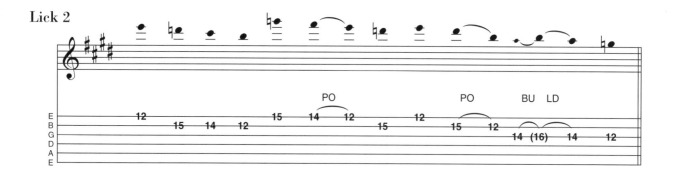

Chuck Berry Solo

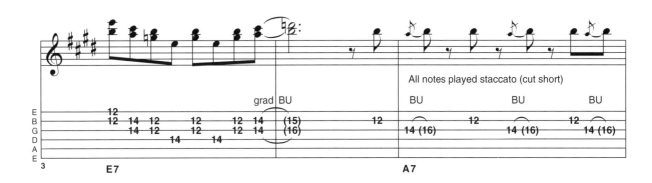

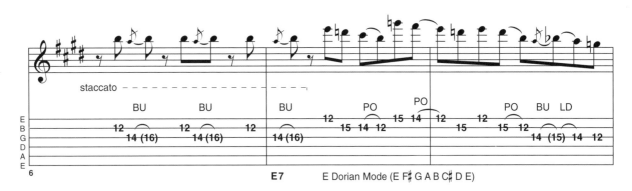

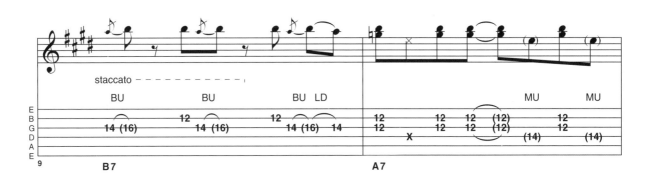

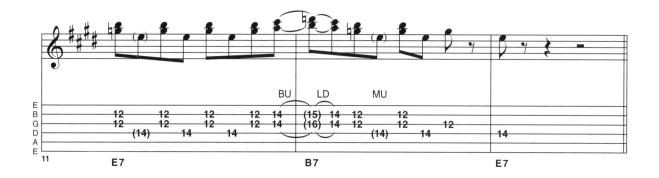

eric clapton
The perfect player

BORN	*30 March 1945, Surrey England.*
DIED	–

That a white English boy could become the most famous blues guitarist ever, would have seemed impossible when Eric Clapton's grandparents bought a guitar for the boy's fourteenth birthday.

Eric immediately set about copying his blues heroes, including BB and Freddie King. Early bands The Roosters and Casey Jones And The Engineers preceded a flash of chart fame with The Yardbirds. But it was his short stint with John Mayall's Bluesbreakers that showed Clapton's true blues spirit.

On *Bluesbreakers*, Mayall gave Eric free musical rein and obtained extraordinary results from the young guitarist. Tracks such as 'Hideaway', 'Double Crossing Time' and 'Have You Heard' showed a master in the making, earning Clapton the nickname 'God'.

His next band was Cream, a three-piece famed for extended improvisations developed through lack of material, rather than artistic desire.

After Cream's split came other short-lived projects: supergroup Blind Faith, a stint with US good-time band Delaney And Bonnie, and a group that was intended to conceal his infamous identity, Derek And The Dominos. 'Layla', Eric's ode to George Harrison's wife Pattie, was a surprise hit from the album *Layla And Other Assorted Love Songs*.

During the 1970s Clapton's life descended into drug dependency. He became a heroin-addicted recluse who pawned his guitars to feed an escalating habit. After help from his friends, particularly The Who's Pete Townshend, Eric made a faltering recovery, passing through chronic alcoholism on his way to finally becoming clean. His playing at this time was weak and uninspired, as he tried to shake off the twin burdens of heroin addiction and the 'God' tag.

Twenty years later Clapton is a superstar. Releasing one platinum album after another, his playing is rounded and mature in every style, from open-tuned Dobro to the fiery electric blues that made his name over thirty years ago.

Recommended listening
John Mayall's Bluesbreakers With Eric Clapton (Decca).

In their own words
"The first thing that rang in my head was black music; all black music that was R&B or blues orientated. I remember hearing Sonny Terry and Brownie McGhee, Big Bill Broonzy, Chuck Berry and Bo Diddley and not really knowing anything about the geography or the culture of the music. But for some reason it did something to me – it resonated. Then I found out later that they were black; they were from the deep South and they were American black men. That started my education. In fact the only education I really had was finding out about blues."
Eric Clapton, speaking in *Guitarist*, June 1994.

Sound advice
Clapton has used most styles of guitar in his long

TRACKS 43-46

biography

and distinguished career. Beginning with Telecasters in The Yardbirds, he switched to the Les Paul for John Mayall. In Cream it was Gibsons again – ES335s and his famous psychedelic Les Paul SG – before Eric found the Stratocaster, at almost the exact time that Hendrix died.

Eric used his famous 'Blackie' through the 70s and 80s, but has recently switched to his Eric Clapton signature Strats, as well as finding favour once again with Gibson guitars. The old red ES335 is occasionally seen, as well as vintage Super 400s, L-5s and Byrdland jazz-style instruments when he wants to recreate the tones of those eras.

Don't go overboard with overdrive, but keep the guitar sounding sharp and attacking; a hint of slapback or reverb is all you need for that Bluesbreaker tone.

Performance notes

Clapton has always played in 'breathing' phrases, as though the notes are the words and the pauses are to take a breath; this comes directly from singing, or from wind instruments, where the musician needs to play that way to take in oxygen. But it's the most expressive and human way to communicate music and guitarists could do worse than emulate it.

This track features the Gibson Les Paul set for a 'clean but distorted' tone. If you want to get that authentic Bluesbreakers feel, imagine you're having a huge row with your guitar; your solo is this argument, with both parties wrenching everything from the opposition. In the end, of course, you kiss and make up.

This and the next three chapters' tracks are all slow blues; listen to each one and see how the different players – Clapton, Green, Hendrix and Page – cope with similar musical scenarios.

STYLE NOTES

- Wide, even vibrato.
- Main scale: G minor pentatonic (G B♭ C D F G).
- Frequent use of large bends.

Eric Clapton Licks

Lick 1

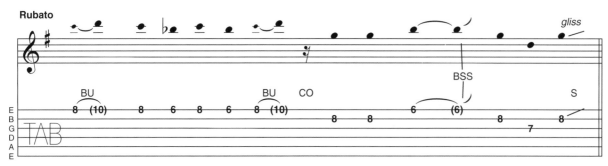

Lick 2

Eric Clapton Solo

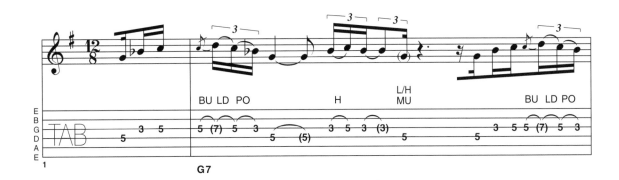

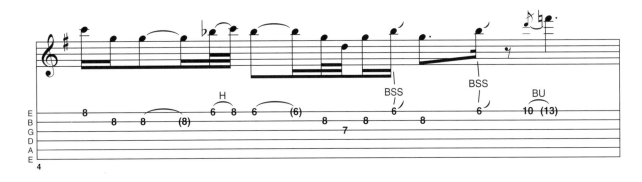

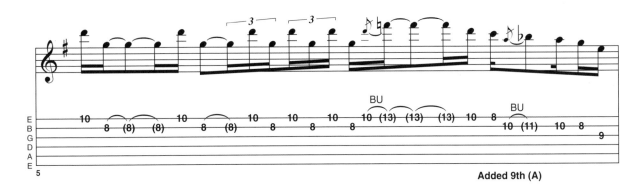

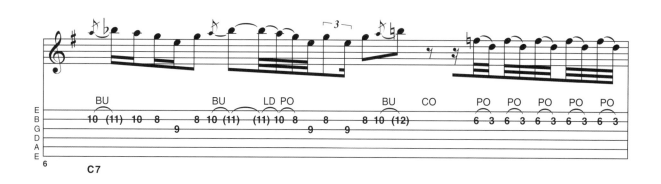

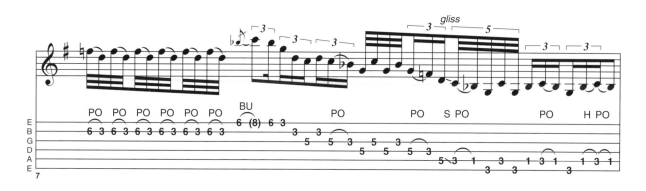

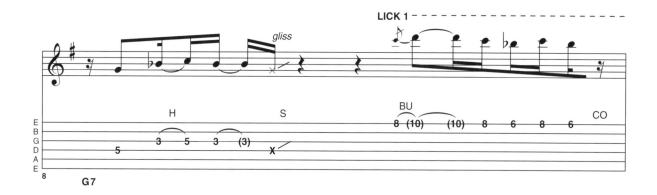

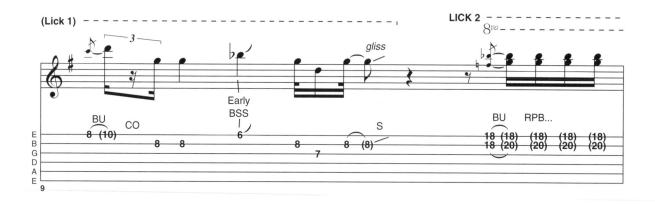

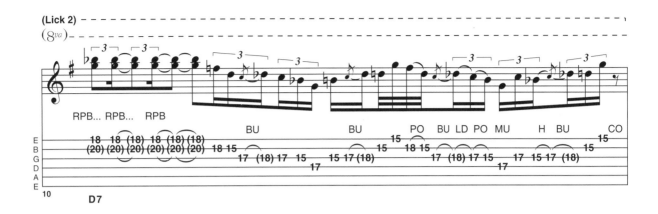

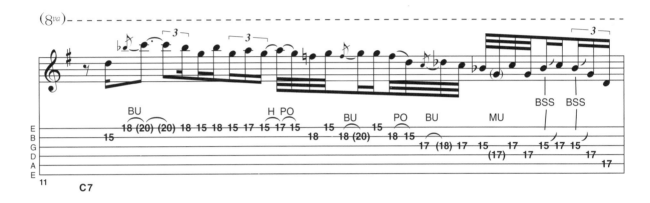

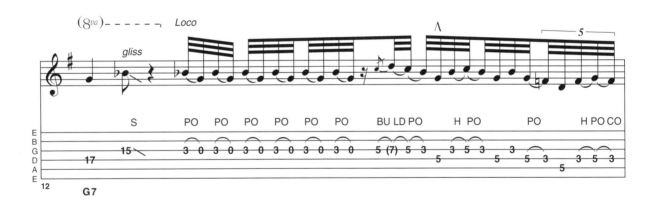

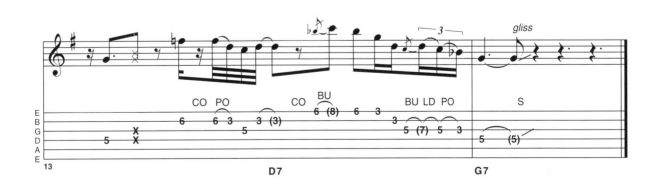

peter green
Feel's true master

| **BORN** | 29 October 1946, London England. |
| **DIED** | – |

When Peter Green stepped into the shoes of John Mayall's former guitarist, Eric Clapton, few imagined the young Eastender would cope so well.

A self-confident character, Green had angled for the job for ages, and when Clapton went 'awol' in 1965, he quickly filled the breech. After God's second going, Peter was hired full-time.

His initial task was daunting; to play the solos made famous by Clapton in front of an audience pining for their hero. But he rose to the challenge, making those solos his own or introducing new songs which the fans came to love. *A Hard Road* showcased Green, with tracks like 'Someday After A While' and 'The Stumble' showing exactly what he could do. Peter's superb compositions, 'The Supernatural' and 'The Same Way' provided a hint as to what would come next.

Just like Clapton, Green used Mayall as a stepping stone to personal goals and was soon forming his own band with John McVie (Mayall's bassist), Mick Fleetwood on drums and eventually two further guitarists, Jeremy Spencer and the precocious Danny Kirwan.

First releases were pure blues; 'Black Magic Woman' and 'Need Your Love So Bad', but following singles showed not only Green's writing skills but a growing introspection. Peter was uncomfortable with making so much for what he saw as so little, and when, allegedly, some bad acid sent him into further decline, he left the band to live a hermit's life for the next twenty-five years. Some pleasant albums were made in the late 70s/early 80s, but Peter would not return to the stage until 1996.

Today, he is back in business. Although not the brash young upstart of yore, Peter grows in confidence with every show and thousands of blues fans are glad to know that Greeny's back.

Recommended listening

A Hard Road (John Mayall, London).

In their own words

"Peter was a very big inspiration. In fact, if it wasn't for him things would be a lot different. He heard Skid Row when we were opening for Fleetwood Mac in Dublin and he invited me back to his hotel afterwards, to jam. He was my big idol at the time and just to meet the guy was enough. And then to have him say I was the best guitarist he'd ever played with; I was walking on air for about six weeks. Then he got his manager to get us a record deal, so I've got a lot to thank him for. Listen to the *Fleetwood Mac Collection* and Peter's sound hasn't dated at all, because he went for a classic blues tone. If you listen to it now, it really stands up."

Gary Moore, speaking in *Guitarist*, March 1989.

Sound advice

As Gary Moore has said, Peter's sound was generally less aggressive than that of Eric Clapton, but there were various particular tones that we associate with him. First is the famous Fleetwood Mac out-of-phase sound that Peter produced by selecting the middle switch position on his old Les Paul. One pickup had been wired out of phase by accident and, with both on together, gave a strange, 'vowely' sound. This is the 'Need Your Love So Bad' tone.

In The Bluesbreakers, Peter tended to use either the treble pickup, or both pickups of his Les Paul together – this was before the 'modification' that made it sound so different. Think of 'The Stumble' and you'll hear a thinnish Les Paul tone with a little echo; it cuts though the backing beautifully.

Performance notes

But there was another Green sound, and this is the one he used on slow minor blues, like the one featured here. Drenched in reverb, the tone is pure, with just a hint of natural drive, a lot of treble and middle but not too much bass. Peter liked spring reverb, so turn your amp's control up to about seven and start feeling sad!

In this type of blues, Green rarely used much vibrato, although his vicious wobble found its way onto many other styles of solo. This shows a musician tailoring his playing to the needs of the track. Peter did it instinctively, but we can all learn from his example.

STYLE NOTES

- Smooth, flowing feel.
- Main scale used: A minor pentatonic (A C D E G A).

Peter Green Licks

Lick 1

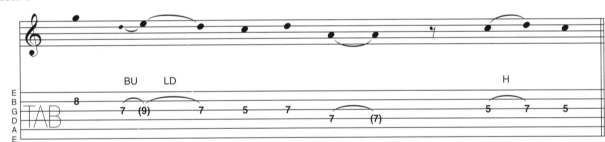

Lick 2

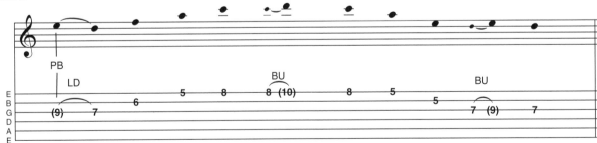

Peter Green Solo

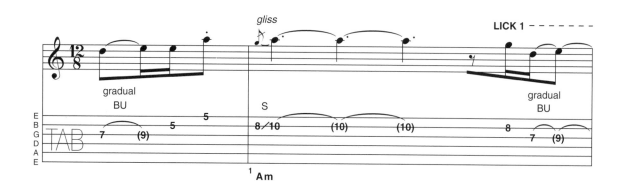

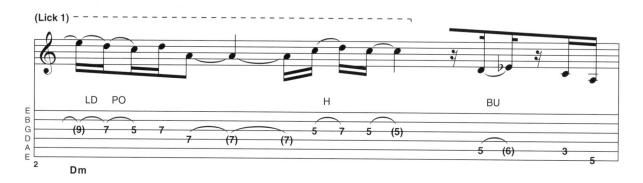

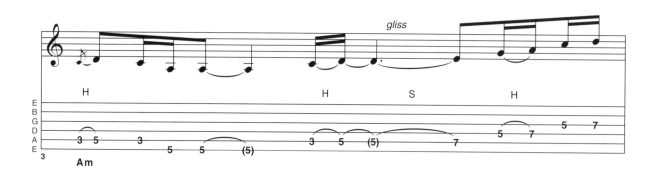

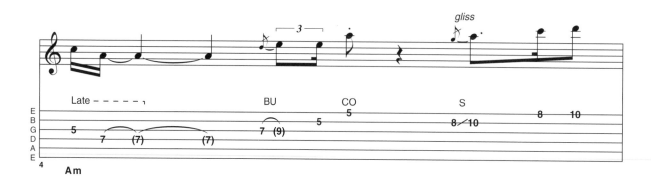

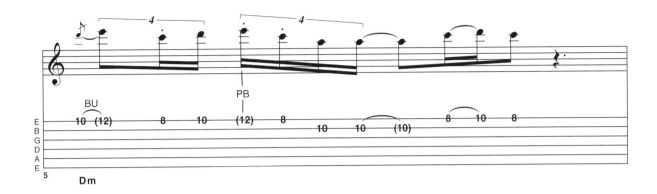

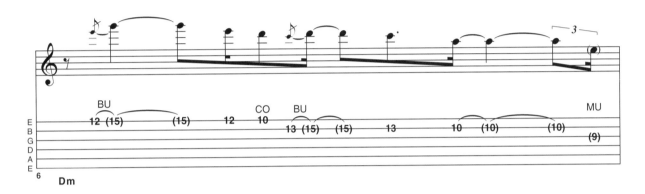

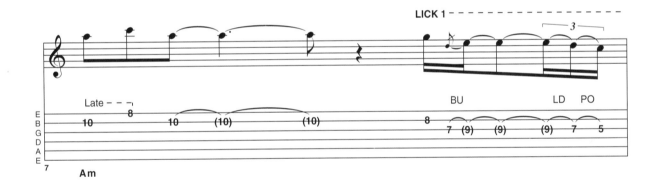

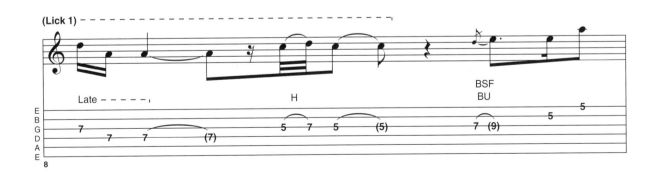

Outlines D minor arpeggio . . .

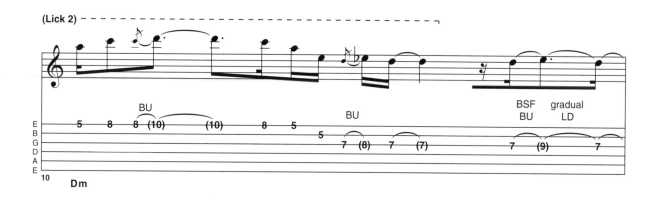

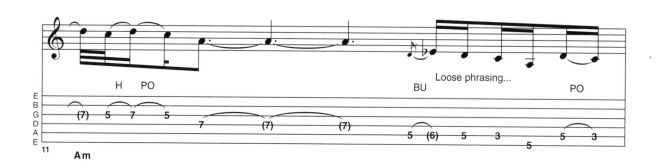

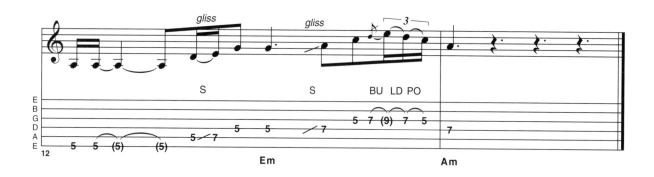

jimi hendrix
More than a purple haze

BORN *27 November 1942, Washington USA.*

DIED *18 September 1970.*

TRACKS 51-54

If Clapton was deemed radical by blues fans, then what would they make of James Marshall Hendrix?

Like Clapton, young Jimi was a fan of blues and immersed himself in learning the licks of heroes like BB King and Buddy Guy. In the early 1960s, after a spell as a US paratrooper, he joined a series of black R&B bands as back-up guitarist. But working with Little Richard, The Isley Brothers and Curtis Knight was musically limiting, so Jimi moved to New York, where he was 'discovered' by The Animals' manager Chas Chandler.

Inviting Hendrix to London, Chas apparently secured his agreement after assuring Jimi that he'd meet Eric Clapton. On his arrival, Jimi sat in with all manner of bands – including Cream – and stunned everyone who heard him play – including Clapton.

With Noel Redding on bass and drummer Mitch Mitchell, The Jimi Hendrix Experience was formed. The first single, the traditional blues 'Hey Joe' was a Top Ten hit, followed by a string of psychedelic tracks, the best of which are 'Purple Haze', 'The Wind Cries Mary' and 'All Along The Watchtower'.

Hendrix's live shows were a visual and sonic assault, but Jimi's 'wildman' image was taking over. It became impossible to concentrate on the music, since the public expected greater outrage with every show – burning or smashing his guitars was becoming passé. Perhaps Jimi's greatest live moment was Woodstock, where he silenced the huge crown with a stunning performance.

Although only four albums were released during his lifetime, bootlegs and unofficial compilations abound. Today, however, Jimi's music is back in the hands of his family and new, improved versions of the original albums are available, plus quality masters of previously unheard material.

Like Marilyn Monroe and James Dean, Jimi's untimely death, choking on his own vomit after taking sleeping pills, ensured perverse immortality.

Recommended listening

In The West (Polydor).

In their own words

"First time I ever met him, we were playing at the Central London Polytechnic and Jimi came along with Chas Chandler. I don't know how long he'd been over here, maybe a couple of days, but he got up and played. He was doing Howlin' Wolf songs and I couldn't believe this guy. Part of me wanted to run away and say, 'Oh no, this is what I want to be – I can't handle this.' And part of me just fell in love. It was a very difficult thing for me to deal with, but I just had to surrender and say, 'This is fantastic!' I got very jealous of Jimi. I was very possessive of him when he was alive and then I got even more possessive. I don't know how long the healing process is, but it's taken me this long to be able to pick up a guitar and play a Hendrix song."

Eric Clapton, speaking in *Guitarist*, June 1994.

biography

Sound advice

Although Hendrix's blues had a lot of power – Marshall amps turned flat out, with various tone-shaping devices thrown in – he generally managed to sound fuzz-free. A lot of this was to do with turning down the guitar to clean things up, but Jimi's touch was so clean and gentle that he managed to retain clarity in everything he did. So, don't go mad with the gain control, add some reverb and maybe the slightest touch of delay to create the live 'stadium' vibe. Just turn the guitar right up when it comes to the finale.

Performance notes

No, Hendrix didn't always use a Strat and no, he didn't always use a distorted tone. This slow blues, on which I used the neck pickup of the Les Paul, is inspired by live versions of 'Red House' and 'Hear My Train A-Comin''. Jimi would often use a Les Paul, Flying V or even an SG to play live blues, and I think this tone suits the style perfectly.

Take care with the vibrato. Hendrix's was smooth and controlled and showed that, underneath all the fire and brimstone, lurked a master of his craft.

STYLE NOTES

- Main scale used: B minor pentatonic (B D E F# A B).
- Licks often flow smoothly together.
- Frequent semi-tone bends.

Jimi Hendrix Licks

Lick 1

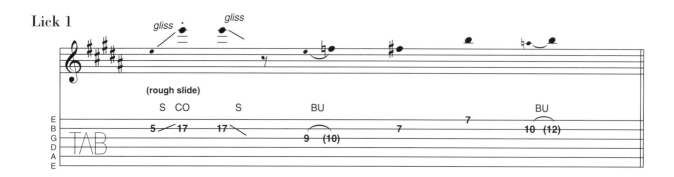

Lick 2

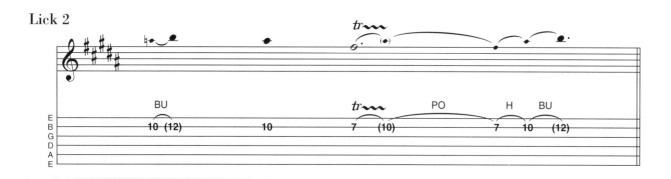

Jimi Hendrix Solo

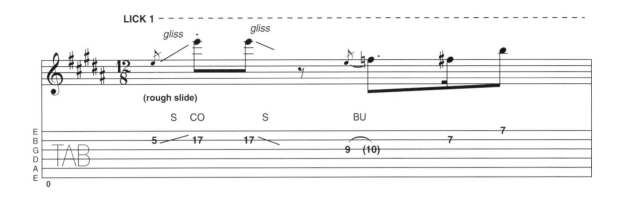

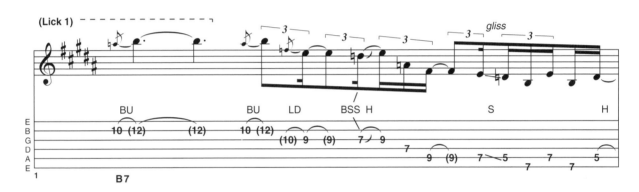

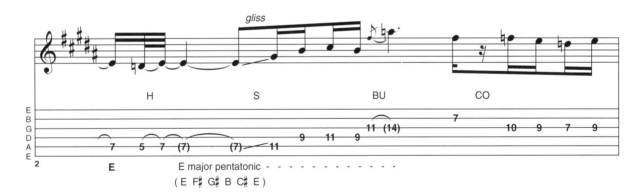

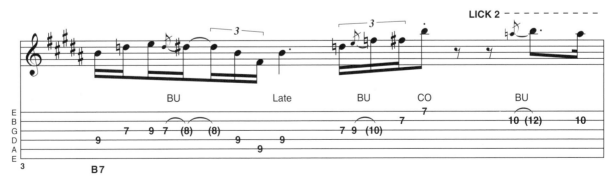

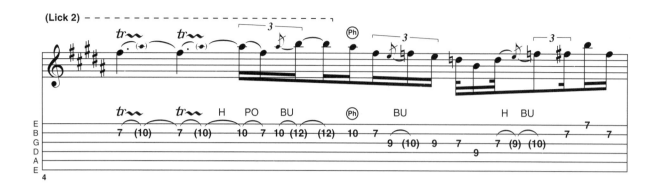

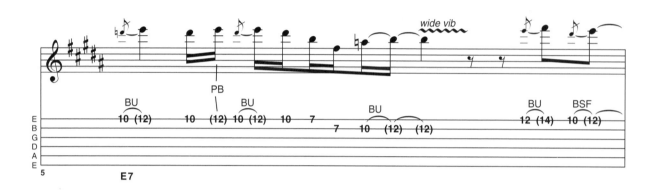

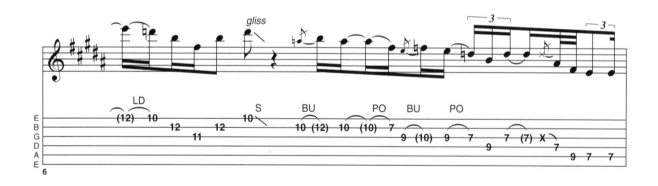

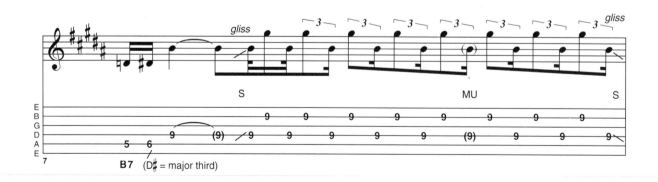

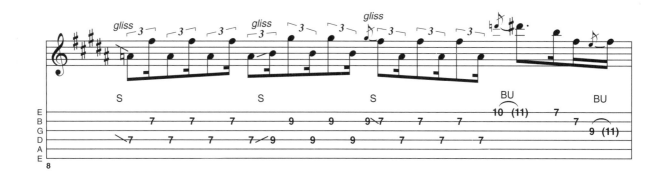

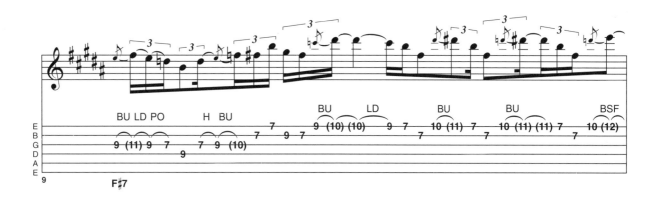

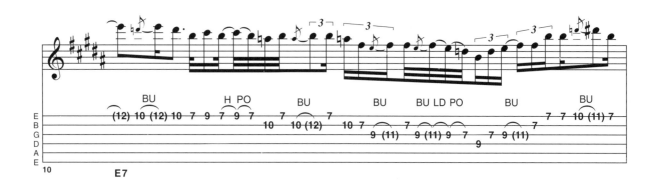

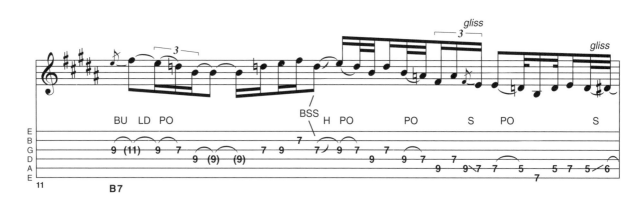

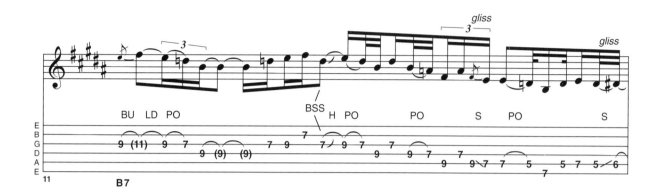

jimmy page
Consummate all-rounder

BORN *9 January 1944, Middlesex England.*

DIED –

Jimmy Page's career reads like a fairy tale. Having learned guitar as a youngster, he soon became adept at most styles of popular music. Influenced not only by blues and rock'n'roll, Jimmy loved the acoustic playing of Davey Graham, Bert Jansch and John Renbourn. His early bands were just friends playing Chuck Berry and Little Richard songs.

His playing career was interrupted when he entered art college. But Jimmy's sights were aimed elsewhere. During frequent visits to London's Marquee club, where he would often sit in, Page honed his blues playing to the point where he was asked to play on a record. That record was 'Diamonds' by Jet Harris and Tony Meehan. It was a Number One smash and Page's career as a session ace was assured.

Along with Big Jim Sullivan, Jimmy ruled the London scene, contributing to countless hit records. Even Page cannot remember which ones, but definite tracks include Dave Berry's 'The Crying Game', Them's 'Baby Please Don't Go' and Joe Cocker's 'With A Little Help From My Friends'.

While attending a gig by The Yardbirds, Page witnessed the virtual break-up of the group; bassist Paul Samwell-Smith walked out and Page offered his services. Rhythm guitarist Chris Dreja soon switched to bass and Page was left playing dual lead guitar with Jeff Beck.

Beck soon quit the band and The Yardbirds decided to split. Page persuaded them that there was work to be had for such a successful outfit and they carried on for a while. When a proposed supergroup, including Page, Beck, The Who's Keith Moon and John Entwistle, plus The Small Faces' singer Steve Marriott, failed to materialise, Page put together The New Yardbirds with session bassist John Paul Jones, drummer John Bonham and vocalist Robert Plant. This group would become Led Zeppelin, the inventors of rock as we know it today. The rest, as they say, is history.

Recommended listening
Led Zeppelin II (Atlantic).

In their own words
"I just kept getting records and learning that way. It was the obvious influences at the beginning: Scotty Moore, James Burton and Gene Vincent's guitarist Cliff Gallup. Those seemed to be the most sustaining influences until I began to hear blues guitarists Elmore James, BB King and people like that. Basically it was that mixture of rock and blues. I wasn't playing anything properly. I just knew a few bits and pieces of solos and things. Not much."
Jimmy Page, speaking to *Guitar Player*, July 1977.

Sound advice
The biggest mistake that people make with Page is the overuse of distortion or overdrive in trying to emulate his tone. Jimmy was a natural player, whose tone was also natural; gained by running straight into his non-master volume amps and letting the Les Paul, or Telecaster, or Danelectro

biography

do the business. You almost never hear fuzz in his studio recordings.

The best way to achieve this sound is to back off the gain on your amp to about half way, push up the master volume to the maximum the venue (or the neighbours) will allow, and go for it.

Reverb and slapback echo will help give that 'immediate', urgent tone that Jimmy played off so brilliantly.

Performance notes

Don't worry about dead accuracy here, but go for feel; be risky; try things you've never tried before and, like Jimmy Page, some of them will come off to great effect.

I've chosen the Les Paul again, using both pickups but with the neck unit turned down to about seven, for a sharp but fat sound. This was a

single take (as were all the solos on this CD) and I did what Jimmy would do and just 'went for it', not worrying too much about accuracy, but going for the feel. Jimmy often uses quick flurries of notes and repetitive licks, and goes for things that he's not sure will come off. Do the same; be risky; try things you've never tried before and, like Jimmy Page, some of them will work just great.

STYLE NOTES

● Main scale used: E minor pentatonic
 (E G A B D E).

● Wide bends (up to four frets).

● Longer and more complex licks than many blues players.

Jimmy Page Licks

Lick 1

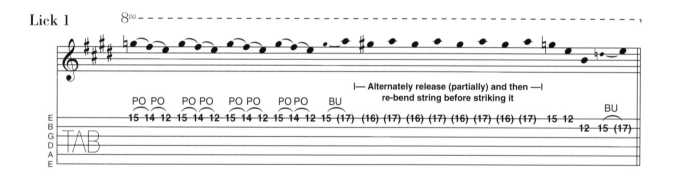

Lick 2

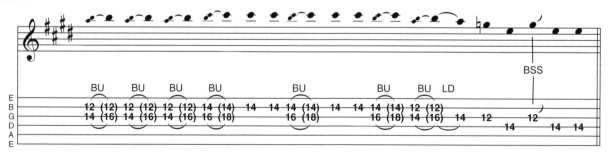

Jimmy Page Solo

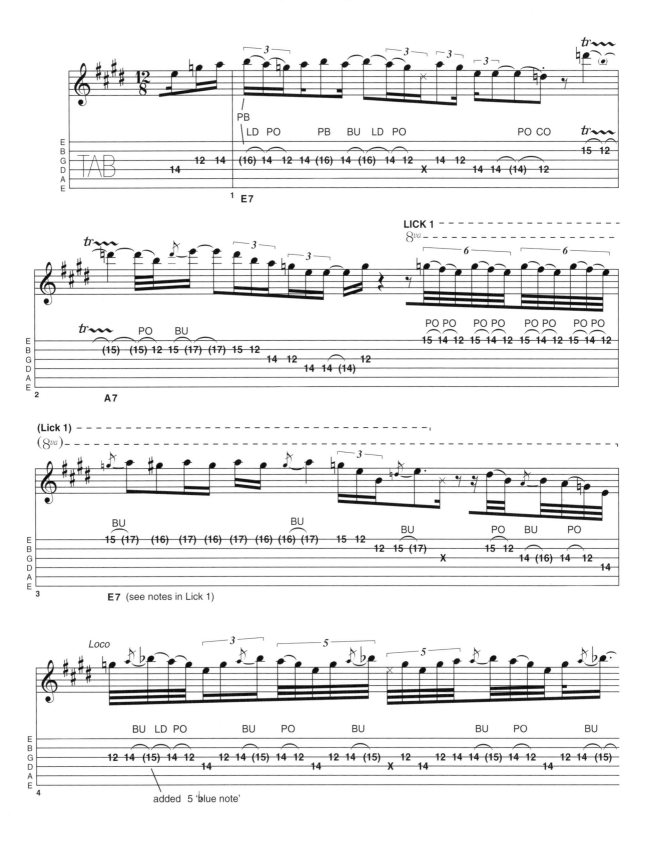

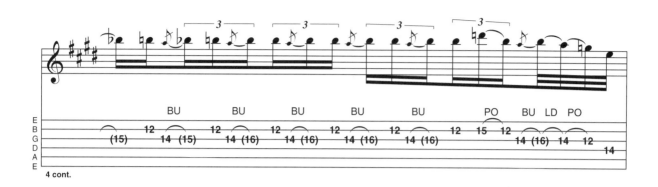

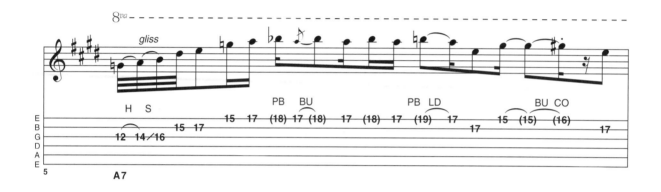

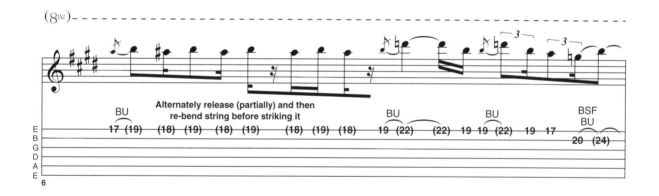

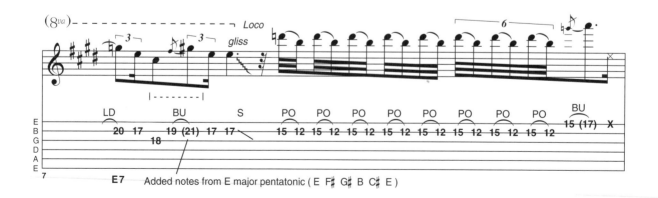

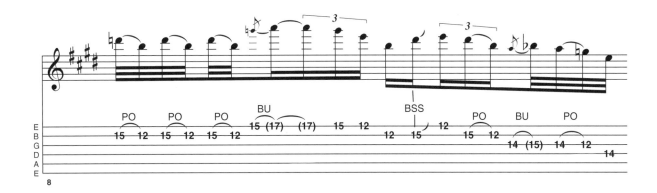

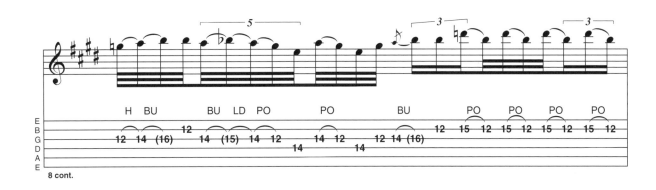

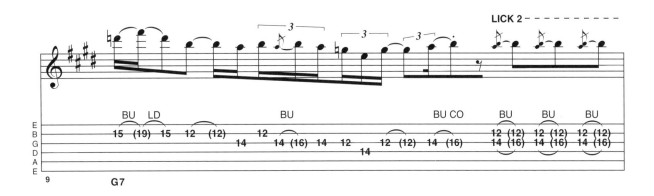

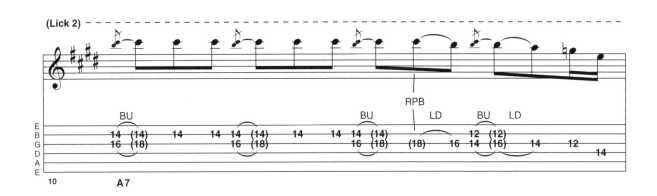

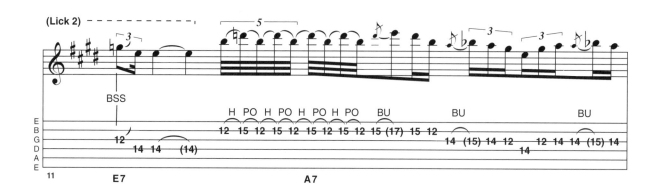

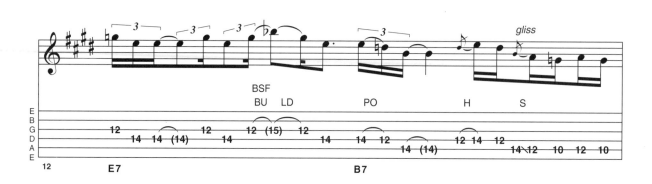

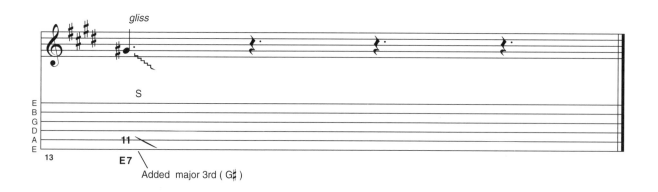

paul kossoff
The wasted talent

> **BORN** *14 September 1950, London England.*
>
> **DIED** *19 March 1976.*

TRACKS 59-62

Kossoff's band, Free, which he formed with singer Paul Rodgers, drummer Simon Kirke and Andy Fraser on bass, launched itself onto the British blues-rock scene in the late 1960s with a fine first album, *Tons Of Sobs.*

This young band contained a wealth of talent, including one of the best rock vocalists ever, a fine drummer and a virtuoso bassist. Kossoff, however, was its focal point. His playing characterised by heavy vibrato, searing tone and sub-Clapton-style licks, Paul's every note was wrenched from his guitar as if it were his last. Free's concerts, which included small clubs even after the band's 1970 hit 'All Right Now', were attended by legions of fans besotted by the music and mesmerised by Kossoff. Had Clapton not already received the accolade, Koss's followers may well have dubbed him God.

The son of actor David, Paul Kossoff learned classical guitar as a child, but astounded his teacher with his ability to play set pieces by ear, after just a hearing or two. His first band was Black Cat Bones with Simon Kirke, with whom he'd later form Free.

Always a rebel, when faced with money and fame Kossoff was almost bound to turn to drugs. He was hounded by hangers on who fed his habit and lived off his fortune. Dogged by ill-health, the tragic outcome was perhaps inevitable.

Despite massive success – 'All Right Now', 'My Brother Jake' and 'Wishing Well' were all Top Ten hits – Free could not sustain the turmoil within, and split in 1971. Brief reunions did occur, but on the final album, *Heartbreaker*, Kossoff hardly played. Ironically, on 'Wishing Well', their last Top Ten hit, Paul Rodgers handled lead guitar.

A wasted talent, Paul Kossoff died aged twenty-six, on a plane on his way to America.

Recommended listening

Fire And Water (Island).

In their own words

"The hangers-on filled his small house in Notting Hill. They would get him to sign cheques when he didn't know what he was writing. Then those cheques would be taken round the corner to Island Records and cashed on Paul's own royalty account. It was found out after his death that a fortune was dissipated in this fashion. Paul was the perfect victim: he was rich, he was weak-willed and he was friendly. He was at that stage in his addiction where all judgement is gone. He was what every drug pusher dreams about."
David Kossoff, speaking in *Guitarist*, March 1996.

Sound advice

Paul's was a big Les Paul and Marshall tone, gained from using the treble pickup on its own and the amp flat out. Although he often used a Stratocaster in the studio and on stage, this is his most recognised sound. Don't go straight for the gain control. If anything, this will take you away from Paul's tone. Instead, crank up the master volume and all the tone controls, then add drive to taste. You could get away with no effects at all,

biography

but add just the tiniest hint of reverb if you feel the sound is a little dry.

Performance notes

Above all else, one thing typified the Kossoff sound: a fast, stonking vibrato, where Paul rocked the whole guitar with his clenched fist.

Kossoff was great at constructing solos; he'd usually start at the bottom of the neck and work his way up the frets until the final crescendo, where big bends and hooligan vibrato took over. Paul used heavy strings and a high action to achieve his sound and feel, so you may have to put up with a less vigorous tone if you're not prepared to string up with twelve-gauge telephone cables!

This track physically hurt my hand, and even then I couldn't quite attain Kossoff's blistering vibrato. Be careful!

STYLE NOTES

● Main scale used: F# minor pentatonic (F# A B C# E F#).

● Wide fast vibrato.

● Lots of oblique bends (play two notes, bending one while the other remains static).

● Minimalistic range of notes and rhythmic patterns.

Paul Kossoff Licks

Lick 1

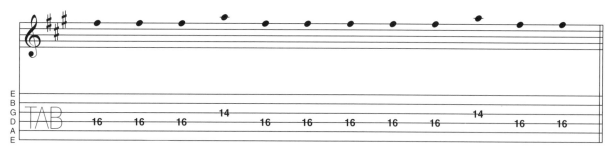

Lick 2

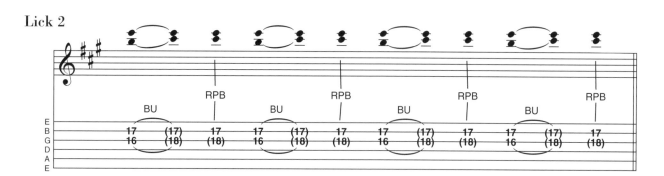

Paul Kossoff Solo

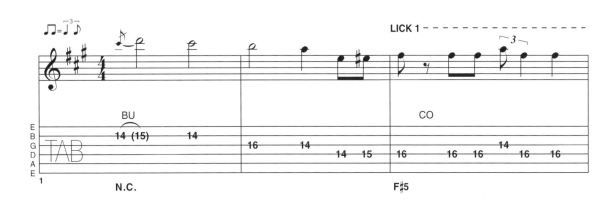

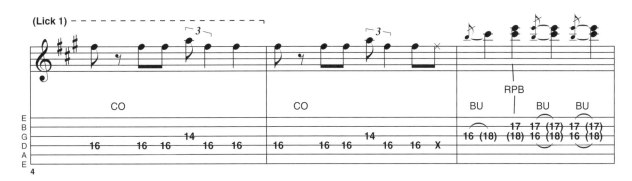

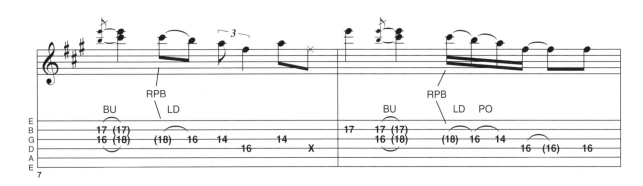

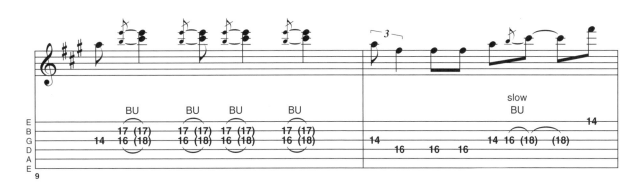

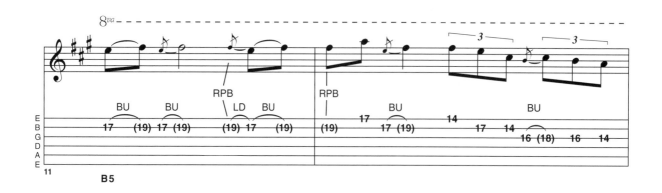

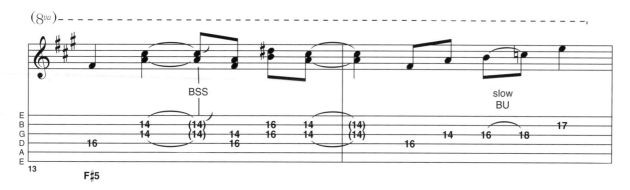

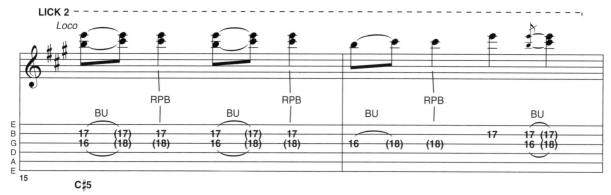

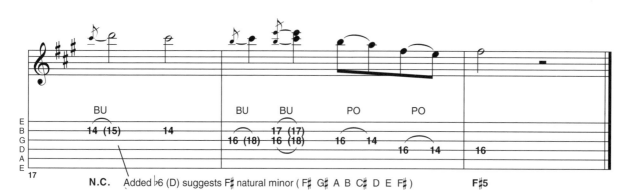

gary moore
Clapton's true successor?

> **BORN** *4 April 1952, Belfast Northern Ireland.*
>
> **DIED** –

TRACKS 63-66

When Gary Moore toured with Skid Row in 1970, onlookers could not believe the skill, fire and speed of the young guitarist. But Moore's career would be as fiery as his playing.

After Skid Row disbanded, Gary formed his own group, but spent time helping out his pals Thin Lizzy (singer Phil Lynott was in the original Skid Row), until he finally joined them in the late 70s. Tenure was short-lived, and Gary left to form G-Force, a rock outfit in which he could demonstrate his flashier side. He also found time to record three albums with Jon Hiseman's high-octane jazz-rock outfit, Colosseum II.

Back in solo mode after G-Force's split, Moore concentrated on writing good rock-pop songs and even made the charts. 'Parisienne Walkways' (with Phil Lynott) was perhaps the first hint of how Gary would eventually break into the mainstream. It was blues, but melodic and technically challenging at the same time, his stunning guitar the real focal point. Two other singles also charted: 'Empty Rooms' and 'Out In The Fields', where he was again joined by Lynott.

Star status came with the exceptional *Still Got The Blues*, which saw Gary returning to his blues roots – he adored Clapton and Green and this record captured that Bluesbreakers essence. *After Hours* followed, with Gary sharing guitar duties with idols Albert Collins, BB and Albert King. *Blues Alive* contained live versions of the previous two albums, before Gary's final blues record to date; a collection of songs from his hero, Peter Green. Although not a huge commercial success, *Blues For Greeny* was a fine tribute from one musician to another. It was also a catalyst for Green's re-emergence.

Gary is currently forsaking the blues in favour of 90s dance music. But don't hold your breath. He'll be back!

Recommended listening
Still Got The Blues (Virgin).

In their own words
"The *Bluesbreakers* album was the *Van Halen* of its day, but more so, because previously there hadn't been anything like it. I just fell in love with the sound of the guitar and ever since then I've loved listening to blues. Eric Clapton quite liked 'Still Got The Blues', because George Harrison told me he'd heard it on the radio and thought it was great. I've met Eric a few times, but I don't really know if he likes what I do. I've seen him play a few times and we've run into each other, but I've never said, 'Hey, do you think I'm great?'"
Gary Moore, speaking in *Guitarist*, March 1992.

Sound advice
Three blues tones typify Gary Moore. First is the Les Paul front pickup with the tone rolled off – Clapton's 'woman tone'. Put the tone back on and you have sound number two, while flicking over to the treble pickup is the third favourite selection.

Gary has favoured Marshall amps in his blues career, linked up to various front-end gain

biography

devices, such as BOSS overdrives and Marshall Guv'nor pedals. Indeed, on 'Still Got The Blues', he used a JTM45, a Guv'nor pedal to smooth things out and an Alesis Quadraverb for that big, wet sound.

Back the treble off your amp (try it at about three) and push the middle and bass controls up. Before adding the overdrive pedal, set up your amp for the Clapton/Kossoff tone and you won't be far off.

Performance notes

Although Gary wrenches the notes from his Les Paul, there's always an over-riding sense of control; he can roll the volume back on the guitar for more subtle moments, before roaring off at full tilt for some devastating legato lick made up from hammer-ons, pull-offs and perfect picking.

For this mid-tempo track I used the bridge pickup of the Les Paul, taking care to spend some time on the lower frets, for that typical 'barking' tone, before continuing up the fretboard. Watch the vibrato; keep it controlled and fluid. Think 'turbo-charged Clapton'. Oh... and unlike me, Gary never fluffs a note!

STYLE NOTES

● Wide vibrato.

● Main scale used: C minor pentatonic (C E♭ F G B♭ C).

● Smooth, 'legato' feel on many licks.

● Wide bends (up to four frets).

Gary Moore Licks

Lick 1

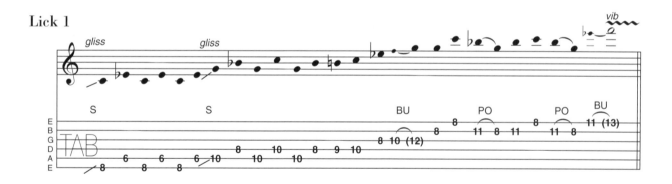

Lick 2

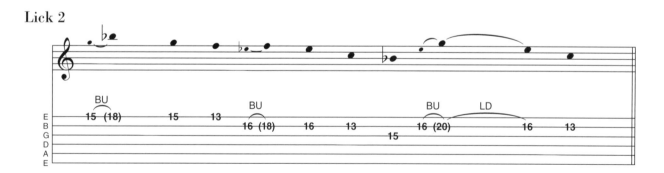

Gary Moore Solo

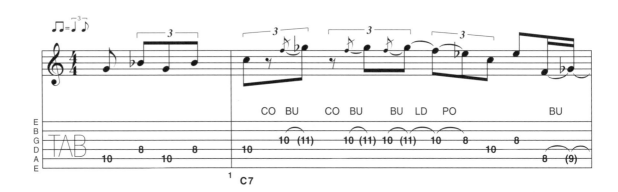

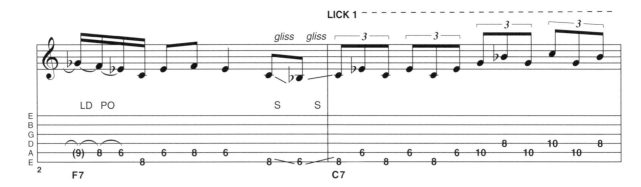

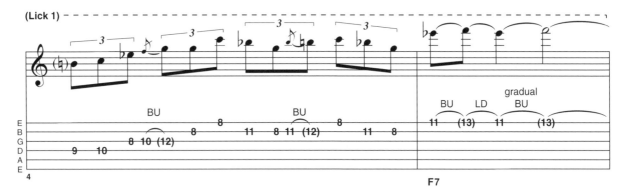

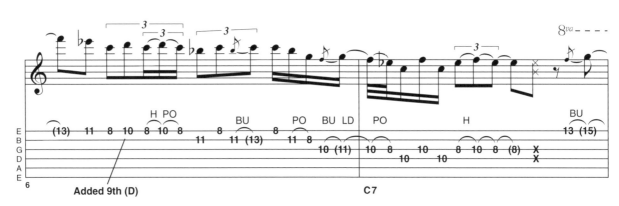

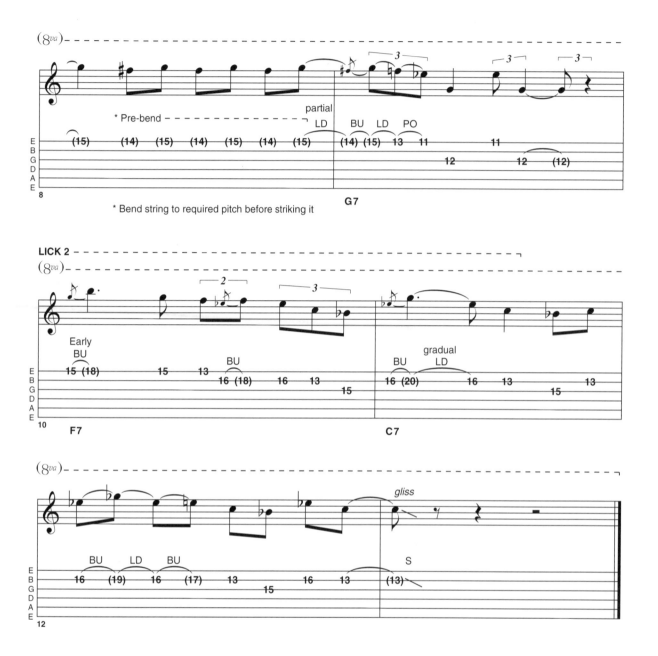

* Bend string to required pitch before striking it

stevie ray vaughan
The Texan tornado

BORN *3 October 1954, Texas USA.*
DIED *27 August 1990.*

In the blues boom of the 80s and 90s, one artist occupied a unique position as an influence over thousands of young hopefuls. With his fiery brand of Hendrix/Clapton-based playing, Stevie Ray Vaughan captivated all who saw him.

Initially the eager pupil of sibling Jimmie, Stevie Ray practised illicitly on his older brother's guitar at every stolen opportunity – he was actually banned from touching it! Initially overshadowed by Jimmie's fame around Austin and Dallas, the young boy quickly developed a formidable technique and was playing in local bars at age thirteen. He was soon the flashier player, but always deferred to his brother's musicianship and professionalism.

By twenty he was recording and at twenty-five formed the band in which he would make his name: Double Trouble, named after the Otis Rush classic. Double Trouble were a permanent fixture on the Texas blues circuit, acclaimed wherever they played. In 1982 they secured a slot at the Montreaux Jazz Festival. Here, Stevie was spotted by David Bowie, who asked him to guest on his album *Let's Dance*. Instant fame followed, but Vaughan turned down the opportunity of touring with Bowie, instead returning to Double Trouble to record the band's seminal album *Texas Flood*.

Although by this time a renowned and sought-after guitarist, Vaughan's life was dogged with drink and drug addiction. In the late eighties he underwent rehabilitation, returning to the blues a refreshed, revitalised and transformed musician.

In 1990, as a guest on Eric Clapton's US tour, he died when the helicopter that was taking him to Chicago after the concert, crashed at East Troy, in Wisconsin.

Perhaps the greatest tragedy of all was that Stevie Ray relished his new-found health, could see the difference it was making to both his playing and his career, and was all set for a meteoric leap forward. How sad then, that we probably never saw the best of this most talented of blues musicians.

Recommended listening
Texas Flood (Epic).

In their own words
"I kept listening, kept going to see people, kept sitting in with people, kept listening to records. If I wanted to learn somebody's stuff, like with Clapton, I learned how to make those sounds with my mouth and then copied that with the guitar. I'd get it to where I could sing it and do it on the guitar at the same time. With Hendrix, I kept trying and trying, and some of the things I just stumbled on to when I was playing. Things would just come to me. It had to do with confidence levels and the excitement of playing, trying new things."
Stevie Ray Vaughan, speaking in *Guitarist*, September 1988.

Sound advice
If you really want to get the Stevie Ray sound

biography

you're going to have to jack up the action on your early 60s Fender Strat, have it refretted with jumbo wire and strung with thirteen-gauge strings. If you're a wimp like me you can get away with slightly lighter strings, but anything less than 10-46 is going to sound a little thin and unconvincing. This is a sound that comes straight from the fingers!

You need a small amp – preferably a non-master volume Fender valve job – that you can turn right up to the max. Then, set your guitar to the front pickup, add the smallest hint of chorus – try the depth and speed controls at around a quarter – and off you go. Some reverb and a dab of slapback echo will give that authentic Texas blues club tone. If the sound is still a little thin, try smoothing it out with a gentle dab of distortion, from something like an Ibanez Tube Screamer or a Rat pedal. Don't overdo it though. Then sling the guitar behind your head and off you go. Have fun!

Performance notes

Apart from his devastating technique, Stevie loved

to push the timing of his notes; laying back until it was almost too late and then coming in at the perfect moment. This was the direct influence of listening to live albums of Jimi Hendrix playing blues.

With a player like this it's hard to teach the nuts and bolt of his style. As Stevie himself did with Hendrix and Clapton, you've just got to listen, listen and listen.

STYLE NOTES

- Main scale used: E minor pentatonic (E G A B D E).
- Frequent bends from minor 3rd to major 3rd (G to G#).
- Minor 3rd often bent only part way to major 3rd.
- Use open position for more robust sound.

Stevie Ray Vaughan Licks

Lick 1

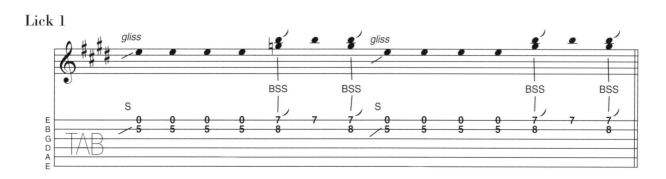

Lick 2

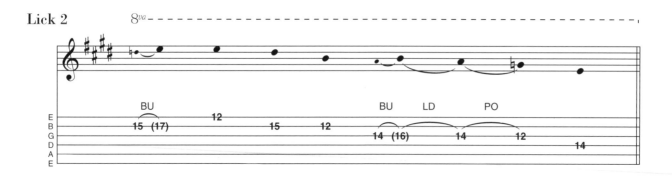

Stevie Ray Vaughan Solo

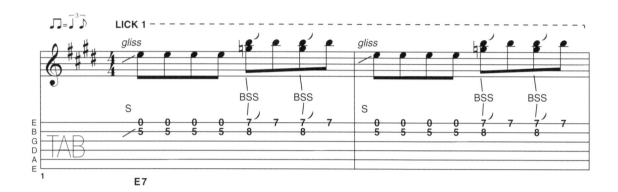

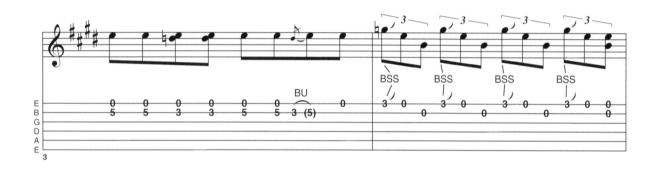

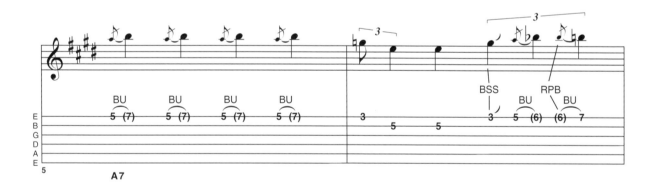

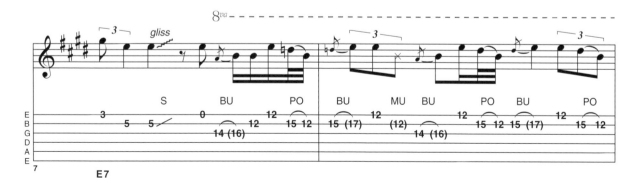

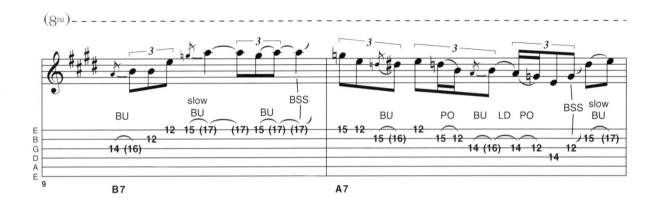

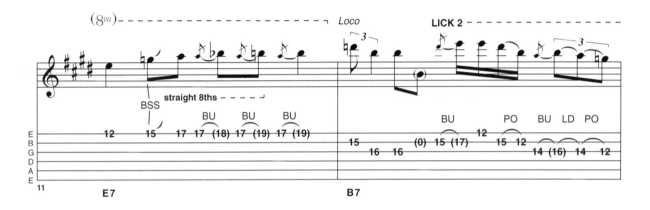

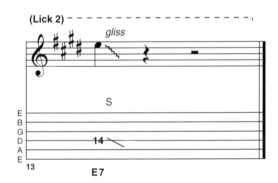

robert cray
Cool dude, hot licks

> **BORN** *1 August 1953, Georgia USA.*
> **DIED** –

Robert Cray is the nearest thing to a black blues pop star that exists. Unless we count John Lee Hooker, that is! His 1987 album *Strong Persuader* catapulted the gifted writer, singer and guitarist to household fame, with its strong selection of songs and tight guitar playing. But Cray had been working in his own band for well over a decade before his 'overnight' success. *Bad Influence* was his first commercial success in 1983, but it was the perfect combination of blues/pop songs, with classic lyrics about illicit love and... well, illicit love, combined with classy guitar playing and singing that ensured the success of *Strong Persuader*.

Cray's influences straddle both the old styles and the new, with strong Buddy Guy and Albert Collins touches to his playing, as well as the more soulful and lyrical guitar voices of Peter Green and even the softer side of Hendrix.

Just as Eric Clapton has managed to find a writing style which perfectly combines pop-rock commercialism with an honest blues feel, so Robert has enjoyed similar success. Indeed, not only has Clapton recorded Cray songs – most notably 'Bad Influence' – but the two also collaborated on the excellent 'Old Love'; a classic slow blues with a very unclassic chord sequence.

Seen with Eric on his now fabled blues nights at London's Royal Albert Hall, Robert Cray could be heard supplying devastatingly soulful rhythm chops behind whichever guitarist was taking centre stage. And that's the mark of a great blues player.

Although some of Cray's later albums have lacked the punch and conviction of his earlier records, 1997's excellent *Sweet Potato Pie* saw him back on top form, with great songs, fine playing and a maturity with which Robert is happily coming to terms. In Robert Cray the world has a subtly brilliant and musical bluesman.

Recommended listening
Strong Persuader (Mercury).

In their own words
"Everyone has their own approach to how they tackle a guitar. A lot of it has to do with your left and right hands. I use my fingers or a heavy plectrum and I go for a real hard attack; similar to what Albert Collins does with his bare thumb. I pluck and pull the strings as well, and I don't use the tremolo arm on my guitar – I just use my left hand for vibrato to get a nice ringing effect. I shake whole chords too. The Stratocaster has good highs and lows, a good clean sound. I can back somebody up with a nice clean rhythm and, if I want it to, it can cut like glass."
Robert Cray, speaking in *Guitarist*, January 1987.

Sound advice
You'll rarely see Robert Cray without a Fender Stratocaster in his hands. Robert likes glassy tones, with little obvious overdrive but always containing a strong flavour of the guitar he's playing. Often favouring the treble pickup on its own, or the treble and middle pickups together,

biography

Cray's sound is pure and cutting. His silver-green 64 Strat has given way to Fender Custom Shop instruments these days, but that pure Cray tone remains constant.

Effects-wise, Robert tends to steer clear of obvious tone shaping, opting for a bit of chorus occasionally, some reverb and a touch of slapback delay at times. So you'll need to expose your technique to close criticism by playing with plenty of middle and treble – some presence if your amp has it – and the bass control set to taste. But lay off that gain. You'll find that, used with a little confidence, a Fender Strat will sing and sustain without drowning it in overdrive. My old woodwork teacher used to say, "Let the saw do the work." In trying to get that real Robert Cray tone I'd say, "Let the guitar do the work."

Performance notes

Cray's playing owes a little to a broad range of other players; you can probably hear people in there who Robert might say were not direct influences. But that just shows what a complete bluesman he is; taking in other players through his pores, almost.

Cray's vibrato is beautiful; he controls it perfectly, timing it to perfection along with the track. Notewise, it's that old T-Bone legacy again, of course with rather more sophistication and a very un-vintage tone.

STYLE NOTES

- Main scale used: C minor pentatonic (C E♭ F G B♭ C).
- Added 9th (D), often accessed by bending up from root note (C).
- Funky feel due to clipped notes and offbeat rhythms.

Robert Cray Licks

Lick 1

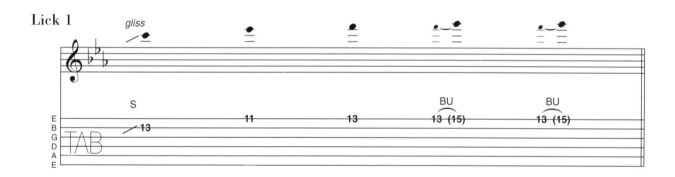

Lick 2

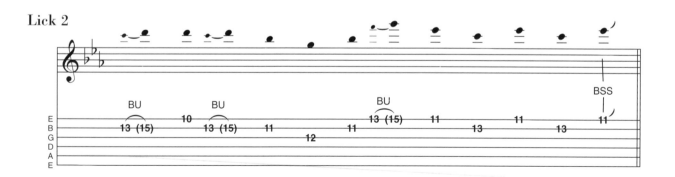

Robert Cray Solo

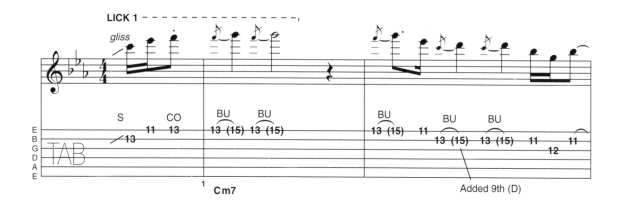

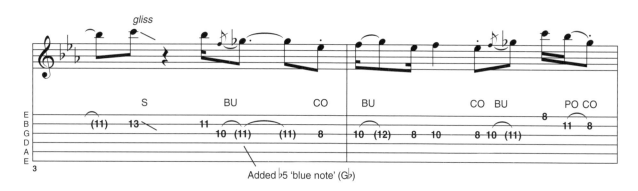

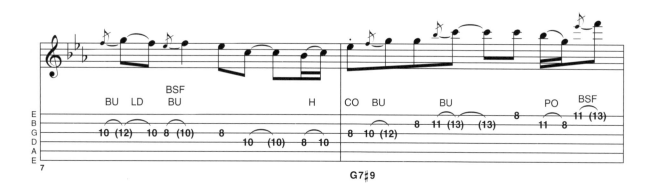

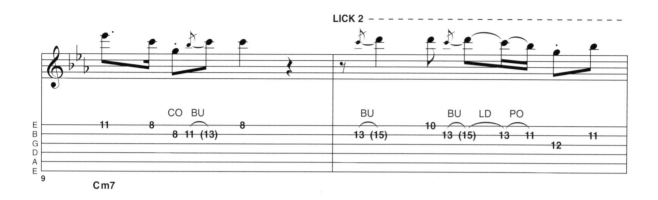

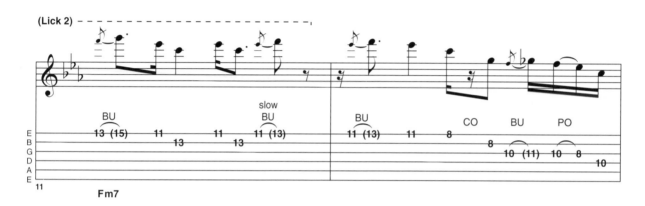

walter trout
Fire and passion

BORN 6 March 1951, New Jersey USA.

DIED –

Walter Trout first came to prominence in John Mayall's band during the mid to late 80s when his ebullient guitar style helped bring Mayall's music back to a wider and more appreciative audience. The night he had to cover as frontman for a sick Mayall, a promoter and record company man just happened to be in the audience. After a ragingly successful gig, the record company man offered a record deal and the promoter suggested he could get Trout work with a band of his own.

Initially a child harmonica and trumpet player, Trout's fumblings on his brother's acoustic guitar became serious when he heard The Beatles. He quickly graduated to an electric instrument and, when he heard Paul Butterfield, with Elvin Bishop and particularly Mike Bloomfield on guitar, he knew he'd found his true vocation.

From there he delved back to the roots of blues, listening to Muddy Waters, Howlin' Wolf and BB King. In his earliest bands, due to a plethora of guitarists and a dearth of singing harmonica players, Walter always ended up on harp and at the microphone. Of course, this would stand him in good stead later on. A stint with John Lee Hooker was a perfect lesson for the aspiring bluesman.

In 1989 he left Mayall and put his own group together. His first solo outing, *Life In The Jungle*, featured a strong set of songs and some stunning guitar work. Great things looked like they were about to happen – indeed, Trout looked like becoming the next Stevie Ray Vaughan. But always more of a live act than a recording artist, Walter subsequently struggled to transmit his raw stage presence to record and his albums have been met with mixed success.

Fortunately, 1997's *Positively Beale Street* was a fantastic recording, showing maturity and power in a fine album of songs. Let's hope it stays this way.

Recommended listening

Life In The Jungle (Provogue).

In their own words

"My brother came home with the Paul Butterfield album that had Mike Bloomfield playing on it. I'd never heard anyone play guitar like that. I'd heard The Beatles, the Stones and all that stuff, but I'd never heard anyone play like Bloomfield. So my brother and I started getting more into blues – Muddy Waters, Howlin' Wolf and BB King. But it was that first Paul Butterfield album that really turned my head around. And I realised I wanted to play that kind of music for the rest of my life."

Walter Trout, speaking in *Guitarist*, November 1991.

Sound advice

Walter's 1974 Fender Stratocaster has been his principal musical tool since he bought it new. He combines it with a Mesa/Boogie combo for a big, punchy tone. There's a feisty middle and top-end grunt to Walter's sound, aided no doubt by his Boogie's powerful gain stages and single 12"

biography

speaker. While the Trout tone is often packed with overdrive, you can always hear the personality of the player and the instrument in anything that he commits to record.

Performance notes

Like most guitarists these days, different Trout tracks often require different tones, different effects set-ups and a different approach. Live, though, Walter tends to stick to the basics, so here I've kept to the bridge and middle pickups together. The Marshall preamp is set with bags of drive, not too much bass, but enough middle and treble to push the sound over the music without

being harsh.

You have to remember that a player's approach – his attack and his touch – affect the sound quite markedly. Walter plays hard, so dig in a little more aggressively than usual. Although the Strat tones are different, notice the similarity between this and the Stevie Ray Vaughan track.

STYLE NOTES

● Licks often feature short burst of speed.

● Main scale used: A minor pentatonic (A C D E G A).

Walter Trout Licks

Lick 1

Lick 2

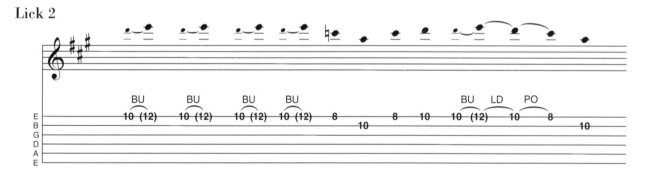

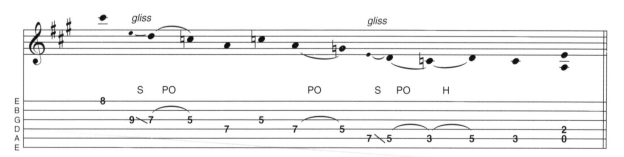

Walter Trout Solo

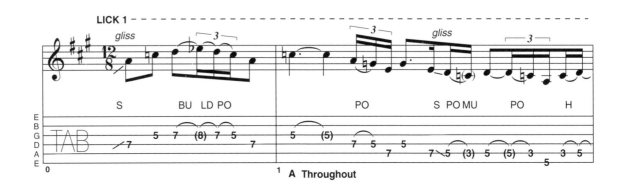

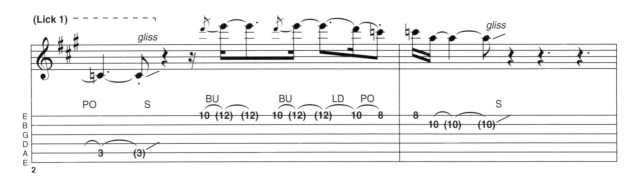

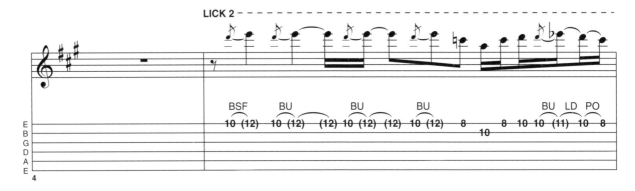

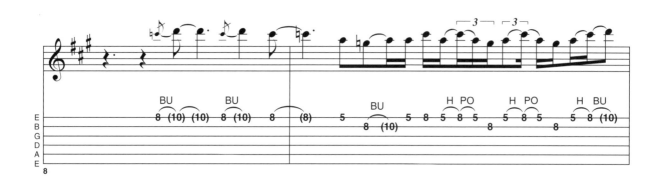

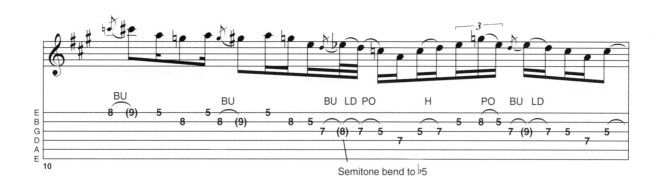

Semitone bend to ♭5

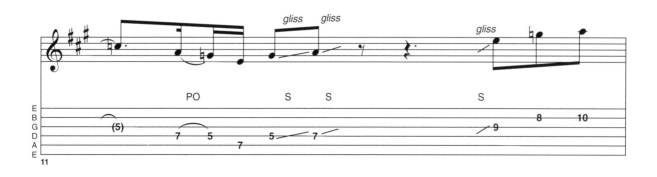

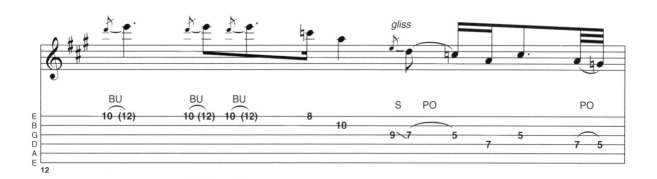

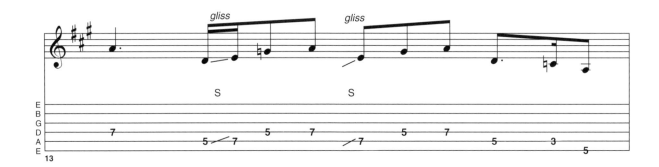

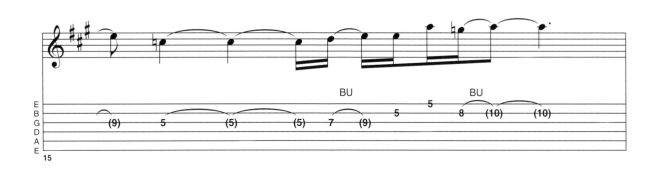

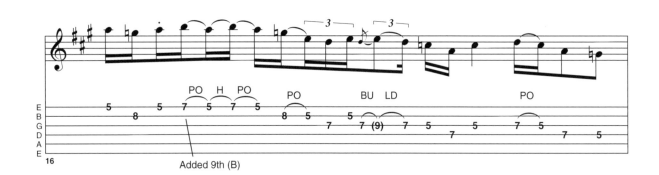

robben ford
Thinking man's blues

TRACKS 79-82

blues

> **BORN** *16 December 1951, California USA.*
>
> **DIED** –

There's no doubt that Robben Ford is among the most sophisticated guitarists around today. His brilliant ability to make simple-sounding blues lines sound complicated and complicated ones sound simple, is the product of true musical knowledge. Indeed, in this book Ford surely ranks as the most musically adept player, by some considerable margin.

Born into a musical family – his brothers Mark, Charles and Patrick are all fine musicians – Ford has had a glittering musical career. Although having played with straight bluesers such as Charlie Musselwhite, Robben also spent time backing Barbra Streisand in LA Express, worked with the incredible Joni Mitchell and even played with ex-Beatle George Harrison. But it's his formation of American jazz group The Yellowjackets that gave him true recognition and led to his work with jazz giant Miles Davis. Few bluesmen can claim such a stunningly impressive CV.

In the late 80s he returned to the blues with a truly outrageous album, *Talk To Your Daughter*, on which he displayed the fire, musicality and wondrous tone that epitomises him today. Live, Ford is a treasure to behold, his lead lines flowing freely around chord progressions which perfectly straddle the divide between blues and jazz.

In an interview with Robben for *Guitarist*, he was most put out when I described his playing as 'Larry Carlton-esque'. Ford was quick to point out that it was in fact the young Carlton who'd adopted his style. I remain suitably admonished.

Recent albums *Robben Ford And The Blue Line* and *Tiger Walk* have shown more of that same guitaristic flair, albeit in rather less salubrious creative surroundings than on the immensely satisfying *Talk To Your Daughter*.

Robben Ford is a true musical giant whose abilities extend far beyond that of the simple blues format. But long may he avail us of his huge talent.

Recommended listening
Talk To Your Daughter (WEA).

In their own words
"My background was pop music and blues. My first guitar inspiration was actually Mike Bloomfield from The Paul Butterfield Blues Band. I also really liked Eric Clapton and Jimi Hendrix, so to me those three were the outstanding guitarists of that era. It wasn't long after listening to those guys that I started hearing people like BB King and Albert Collins; today he is still my favourite blues guitarist.

"Then R&B got very in vogue, with Otis Redding and Wilson Pickett, Booker T And The MGs. In fact, Steve Cropper from The MGs produced my first record, but by the time I got round to doing that, I was playing much more of a jazz fusion style, so he worked on balancing it and keeping it funky. But most of my listening is to jazz; Miles Davis, I'm always listening to Miles Davis."

Robben Ford speaking in *Guitarist,* October 1988.

biography

Sound advice

Ford's Dumble Overdrive Special amps with 2x12" Electro-Voice cabinets, and either a Fender Esprit (twin-cutaway, dual humbucker guitar) or Telecaster, provide the tools for the job. When he's playing 'dirty', Robben rarely shifts from the treble pickup.

Coming from the jazz end of the blues, Ford's long, sustaining notes and smooth runs rely heavily on sustain, with a lot of middle and top end in the tone. Here you can really get to grips with your amp's gain control; whack it up high and then back off until you find the 'sweet spot'; the point where the guitar, the preamp and power amp sing together as a single unit.

Simple reverb should be enough to provide a good, 'live' sound which should help give the fluidity to play like this exciting and talented guitarist.

Performance notes

Apart from perhaps Gary Moore, Robben Ford generally uses more front-end drive than any other player in this book. But there's another side to his playing; sparkly, liquid notes and a pure, clean tone. Surprisingly, perhaps, I've chosen that facet of Robben's style for *Giants Of Blues*.

This fairly jazzy track provides just enough harmonic variation to make simple blues scale or mixolydian licks sound 'musical'. It's the placing of the notes within the bar, not just the notes themselves, which gives much of the Ford feel. Lay back, give yourself time and make each note count. In fact, why not try to do that in all your blues playing. Good luck, and have fun!

STYLE NOTES

- Main scale used: B♭ minor pentatonic (B♭ D♭ E♭ F A♭ B♭).
- 9th and 6th often added to suggest Dorian mode (B♭ C D♭ E♭ F G A♭ B♭: same notes as A♭ major).
- Smooth 'fusion' type feel.

Robben Ford Licks

Lick 1

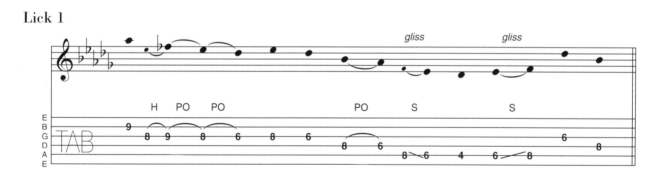

Lick 2

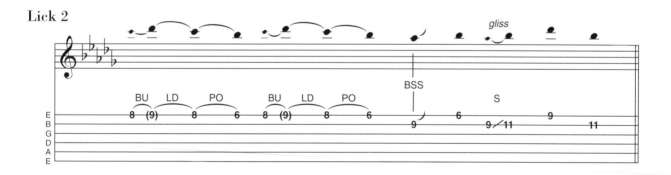

Robben Ford Solo

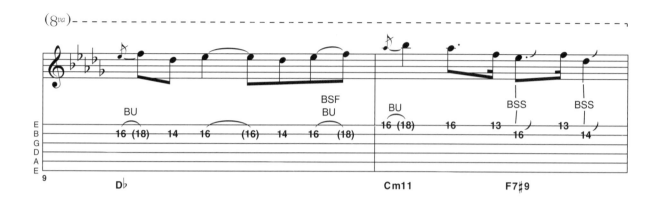

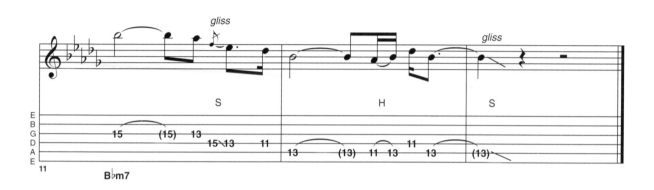

blue guitars

A look at some of the instruments that have become the voices of blues guitar

Although any guitar can be used for any style of music, certain makes and models have a definite association with blues and particular blues guitarists.

Many bluesers have used, or continue to use, more than one type of guitar – Clapton plays Fender Strats, Gibson Les Pauls and 335s, as well as National and Martin acoustics, for instance. So in the following look at blues guitars, don't be surprised to find mentions of the same players in different sections. We begin with perhaps the most widely used blues guitar of all...

Fender Stratocaster

The Stratocaster is perhaps the best recognised electric guitar on the planet today. However, it was not until relatively recently that it has become widely used in blues. On both sides of the Atlantic, many players, most notably Freddie King and Eric Clapton, favoured the power and richness of Gibsons. In comparison with the mahogany and powerful humbucking pickups of a Les Paul or ES335, Strats (and Fenders in general) were viewed as distinctly 'thin' sounding with their single-coil pickups and ash/alder and maple construction. Then, in 1967, one James Marshall Hendrix exploded onto the world scene.

Hendrix is often derided merely as an exhibitionist by those who have never studied his work, yet recordings such as 'Hear My Train A-Comin'' and 'Red House' stand as testimony to his undoubted mastery of blues guitar. His explosive technique, coupled with the unprecedented range of tones he coaxed from his Stratocaster, was enough to convince many that this was the guitar to have. Before long, Peter Green, Eric Clapton and Jeff Beck followed suit.

Fundamental to this shift is the Stratocaster's unrivalled suitability for high-volume use. Rather than becoming more difficult to play at volume, Strats respond extremely well, offering controllable, musical feedback instead of horrible, unruly noise. Some players still find them a little weak, choosing to install humbuckers for fatter, more powerful overdrive. Yet, as far as the blues is concerned, players such as Buddy Guy, Walter Trout and Robert Cray all prefer their Strats pretty much stock. In fact, Buddy Guy is an interesting case in point. While a majority of Chicago blues players were using Gibsons in the early 60s, Guy had used Fenders – although not exclusively – since 1958. His comments sum up the essence of a Strat for many players: "I was always a wild man with the guitar, and when you play like that, the guitar has to be rough. So I went for the Strat."

A hugely significant stage in the Stratocaster's evolution was when Eric Clapton decided to retire his beloved 'Blackie', and asked Fender to build him a new guitar. The result was the Eric Clapton Signature Stratocaster that has spawned a whole range of artist-endorsed instruments, including Stevie Ray Vaughan, Buddy Guy and Bonnie Raitt guitars.

Today Stratocasters are highly collectable – indeed, the most highly prized are those from the pre-CBS period 1954-64, fetching anything up to £15,000. As with many of the guitars featured here, it is striking that these vintage instruments have remained largely unchanged since their inception in the 1950s. While technological developments define and shape virtually every other industry, Leo Fender's Stratocaster from 1954 still looks as though it could have been designed only yesterday.

Not only the number one guitar, but the number one blues guitar in the world

Gibson Les Paul

Right from its inception, Gibson's legendary Les Paul model has been closely associated with the blues. Les Paul himself had been experimenting with a solid-bodied guitar even before Leo Fender introduced the Broadcaster in 1950 (later to become the Telecaster). Gibson was reluctant at first to accept the design, but with the foresight and guidance of resident company genius Ted McCarty, the first Les Paul model appeared in 1952.

Where Fender's main criteria for electric guitar design were function and affordability, Gibson had long prided itself in its superior materials and fine craftsmanship. The Les Paul was no exception, with its striking gold finish. Early Goldtops quickly won the hearts of the Chicago bluesmen, in particular Freddie King, who had such a huge influence on a certain Mr Clapton. Eric had seen Freddie King on the cover of *Let's Hide Away And Dance Away* with what he thought was a sunburst Les Paul. He bought one, used it on *Blues Breakers* with John Mayall, and inadvertently made flame-top Les Pauls the most collectable and desired electric guitars of all time. Clapton used a Les Paul until the early Cream days.

On the other side of the Atlantic, Mike Bloomfield had put down his 52 Tele in favour of the Les Paul that would become his trademark. Through his work with The Paul Butterfield Band, Bob Dylan and his own solo projects, Butterfield helped cement the Les Paul as one of the best blues guitars of all time.

Clapton's Bluesbreaker successor, Peter Green, also used a Les Paul. Where Clapton had experimented with the thick, overdriven tones of a small Marshall amplifier, Peter Green's Les Paul tone – especially by the time he'd joined Fleetwood Mac – was less distorted and often drenched in reverb. Also, after a service, Green's Les Paul came back with a wiring fault which caused the two pickups to work out of phase with one another. The haunting results can be heard on 'Need Your Love So Bad' and 'Stop Messin' Around'.

As the 60s rolled on, more and more guitarists opted for Les Pauls. Jeff Beck manipulated his to almost unbelievable tonal extremes, while Paul Kossoff of Free and Jimmy Page of Led Zeppelin recorded some of the most memorable blues-based rock ever. Throughout the 70s Billy Gibbons of ZZ Top and Duane Allman of The Allman Brothers kept the Les Paul sound alive and well in their own brand of bluesy, southern rock. However, towards the end of that decade, the popularity of Les Pauls waned somewhat on this side of the Atlantic, with the various changes in musical trends. Things changed in the 1980s, when along came Slash of Guns N' Roses, whose bluesy riffs reminded countless guitarists what they were missing. Then towards the end of the 80s, Gary Moore began his retrospective look at the blues with the very guitar Peter Green had used for his own seminal recordings.

Today, flame-top Les Pauls from 1958-60 command some of the highest prices of any vintage guitars, while all Les Pauls are still highly desired by players and collectors alike.

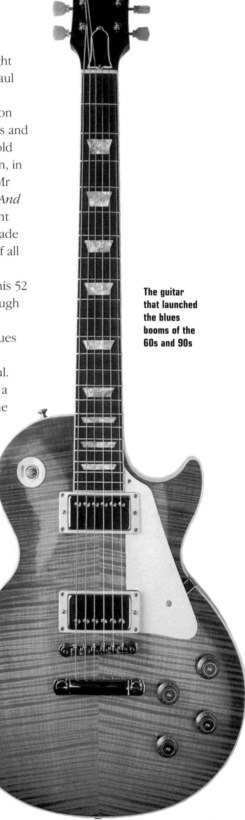

The guitar that launched the blues booms of the 60s and 90s

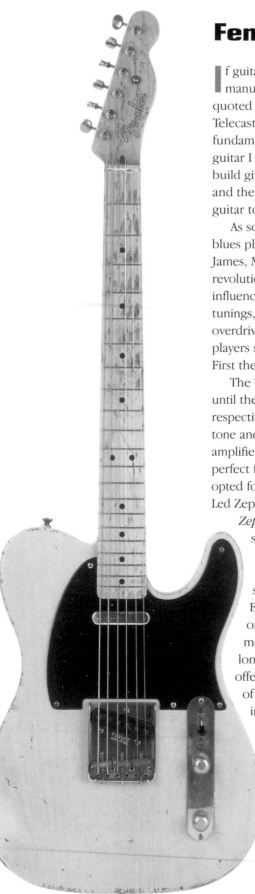

Fender Telecaster

If guitars were cars, Leo Fender was the Henry Ford of guitar manufacturing and the Telecaster was his Model T. An oft-quoted analogy, but undoubtedly true. The remit for the Telecaster was simple, and represented a convergence of two fundamental questions for Leo Fender: how can I build the guitar I want most effectively? And, what is the best guitar I can build given my resources? Well, Leo got it absolutely spot on, and the Telecaster remains as the most functional, workhorse guitar to this day.

As soon as the very first Telecasters left the factory in 1950, blues players such as Clarence 'Gatemouth' Brown, his brother James, Muddy Waters and a whole host of others embraced this revolution in guitar design. It was Clarence's distinctive style that influenced players such as Guitar Slim and Albert Collins; open tunings, extensive use of the capo and volume-generated overdrive. Yet the 50s was a time of huge innovation and many players simply opted for the newest guitars as they came out. First the Les Paul in 1952, the Strat in 1954 and the ES335 in 1958.

The Tele caught on in England, too, although arguably not until the 60s. Both Jeff Beck and Eric Clapton used Teles for their respective stints in The Yardbirds, favouring the guitar's incisive tone and trendy appearance. In the absence of modern, high gain amplifiers, the Telecaster had the ability to cut through, sounding perfect for bluesy playing in a pop format. Later, Jimmy Page opted for a Telecaster on some of his most memorable work with Led Zeppelin. For example, listen to 'Whole Lotta Love' on *Led Zeppelin II*; most people assume that this huge, ballsy sound is a Les Paul, but on closer listening, the guitar's identity comes as a surprising realisation.

Yet in blues as a whole, the Telecaster holds arguably a secondary role to both Fender's Stratocaster and Gibson's ES335. But those players who remained faithful to the original solid-body electric are perhaps some of the most memorable. Four players, three of whom are sadly no longer with us, admirably demonstrated the huge potential offered by the Tele. Firstly, Roy Buchanan, whose melting pot of country, blues and rock simultaneously amazed and inspired countless players. Then there was Wilko Johnson of Dr Feelgood, and of course Irish blues legend Rory Gallagher, who showed the Telecaster's suitability as a slide guitar with astonishing feel and precision. Finally comes Albert Collins, whose breathtaking attack and tone leave you in absolutely no doubt as to the guitar he's playing.

The most basic solid electric guitar produces some of the most musical tones, from Albert Collins to Robben Ford

Gibson Thinline Semis

By 1958, Gibson's Ted McCarty was absolutely flying where guitar design was concerned. After innovations such as the tune-o-matic bridge, among others, he came up with the legendary ES335. To many, it must have appeared as a slight regression after the radical Stratocaster. Yet what he had done, was to take Les Paul's 'Log' to its logical conclusion. Many players still held great affection for big-bodied semis, but had to suffer with excessive feedback and poor sustain. McCarty simply thinned the body down and included a solid timber block through the centre of the guitar which, to a large extent, cured both of these problems. Furthermore, the ES335's twin-cutaways enabled players to access the uppermost frets.

With their new found versatility, coupled with a keen eye on aesthetics of the past, Gibson's new 'Thinline' caught on very quickly with blues players. In particular, one Riley B King. BB has played an ES355-style guitar to this day and now has is own 'Lucille' signature model, complete with bound headstock, fine-tuning bridge and bereft of f-holes. Another King – Freddie – is most commonly associated with stereo ES345s. During the Chicago blues explosion of the mid-50s King, like many others, often used Les Pauls. Yet the 300 series, with its semi-solid design and maple construction, offered the perfect balance between Gibson power and Fender versatility. Freddie never looked back. Buddy Guy, too, although more commonly associated with Strats, holds 335s dear for their rich and full sustain, coupled with unmistakable, cutting clarity. Similarly, John Lee Hooker is famed for his seated renditions of 'Boom Boom' accompanied, of course, by his thinline semi. He now endorses Epiphone guitars.

Then of course, there is Chuck Berry. Influenced strongly by the guitar antics of T-Bone Walker, the image of Berry duckwalking with his cherry red 335 during 'Johnny B Goode' is one of the most enduring depictions of rock'n'roll.

As the 60s rolled on, a new era was about to begin – psychedelia. Absolutely central to this were Hendrix (of course) and Cream. After Eric Clapton's sterling work with John Mayall, he put down his Les Paul and headed for the rather different company of Jack Bruce and Ginger Baker. Although Clapton's main studio guitar was his painted SG, a block-inlaid, cherry red 335 made frequent appearances during the tail end of Cream's short existence. If there's any scepticism surrounding the 335's resistance to feedback, then Eric Clapton lays it to waste on the 'Goodbye Cream' series of performances. More recently, Clapton has been seen with this same 335 at some blues-only gigs.

Today, Gibson still produces the ES335 in various incarnations. Vintage models vary greatly in desirability, but it's the blonde, dot-neck variety from 1958-60 that command the biggest sums – how about £20,000?!

Gibson's most expressive guitar, the ES335 finds favour with the top blues artists

Gibson ES150/250

Gibson's ES150 was developed from the company's L-series archtops, employing an electro-magnetic pickup designed initially for lap-top Hawaiian guitars. It became an immediate success in 1937.

Many players regard the ES150 primarily as a jazz guitar. Yet its effect on electric blues – and the electric guitar as we know it – is hugely significant for two reasons. Not only was it the first guitar to feature a pickup, but that pickup was later to become known as the 'Charlie Christian' – the player with whom it is most commonly associated. As the huge orchestras of Louis Jordan and the like had to downsize to minimise costs, guitarists were promoted from their largely rhythmic role, to front-line status. With new found amplification, Christian exploited the electric guitar's potential, with his flowing, melodic style influencing countless players along the way.

In 1938, Gibson offered a new model, the ES250, featuring a slightly larger body, a compensated saddle and more elaborate binding and ornamentation. Twice the price of the 150, this guitar attracted T-Bone Walker, whose on-stage antics and sophisticated jazz/blues style won favour with Jimmy Witherspoon and Memphis Slim. Walker was one of the first, true exponents of the electric guitar, influencing BB King, Chuck Berry and Clarence 'Gatemouth' Brown among others.

By 1940, demand for the ES250 had waned and it was discontinued. Nevertheless, it had helped form the basis for Gibson's post-war archtop electrics such as the ES300, 350, Super 400 and Byrdland. The electric guitar's potential was recognised outside Gibson, too. Epiphone, in particular, were making archtops of their own, attracting the likes of John Lee Hooker, who remains an Epiphone faithful to this day.

So, despite the huge legacy bequeathed to the jazz world in terms of its revolutionary players, Gibson's ES150 undoubtedly left its own indelible mark on the future of electric blues. Today, original examples are highly collectable, commanding inordinate sums if not for their outright playability and sound, then for their rarity and historical significance.

This modern ES135 is a direct descendant of those early Gibson electric semis

Gibson Explorer/Flying V

Yet another of Ted McCarty's innovations was the Flying V. Introduced in the late 1950s as one of a trio of weird-shaped Korina-wood instruments, these guitars were McCarty's vision of "an asset to the combo musician with a flair for showmanship". Yet, along with its 'Korina Trio' siblings, the Explorer and the bizarre Moderne, the Flying V didn't sell well to a relatively conservative late 1950s America: rock'n'roll was one thing; these were entirely another. Ironically, and as a result of tiny production numbers, late 50s Vs have gone on to become some of the most highly prized and valuable vintage guitars.

Gibson produced a few more Vs in the early 60s in an attempt to use up left-over parts. They subsequently appeared with numerous British pop acts, including The Kinks' Dave Davies – who, incidentally, thought your arm was supposed to go through the vee– and Brian Jones of The Rolling Stones. But it is with blues players that the V's most celebrated heritage lies. Had McCarty seen what was to come, Gibson would surely have persevered: enter Jimi Hendrix. Although famed for his love of Stratocasters, Hendrix often used a Flying V, most notably on 'All Along The Watchtower', or so the story goes. His choice was undoubtedly inspired by blues legend Albert King who, like Hendrix, was left-handed. King played Vs almost exclusively from their debut in 1958, right through to his sad and recent death. He was completely self taught and simply turned a right-handed guitar upside down – without even reversing the strings.

It's astonishing to think that almost all Gibson's most famous electric guitars of the 50s and 60s featured the same pickups and controls: the Les Paul Standard, ES335, SG and the Flying V. What is so surprising is that they all sound very different. In the V's case, the resultant tone was more toppy and cutting than its brethren, yet still retained the inherent warmth and power of the humbucking pickups.

Various rock players, such as Michael Schenker, still use a V, but in blues, it is really only Lonnie Mack who still flies the flag for McCarty's space-age creation. Although not mega-famous, Mack is nonetheless responsible for inspiring Stevie Ray Vaughan, Mike Bloomfield and Eric Clapton among others – none of whom shares his taste in guitars. Strangely, though, Clapton has been seen toting the outlandish Explorer, and its less angular offspring, the Gibson Firebird.

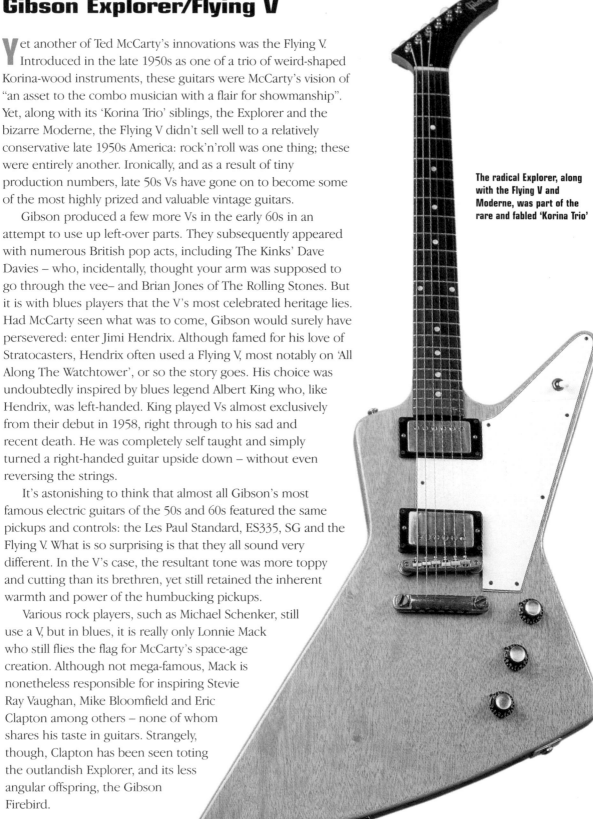

The radical Explorer, along with the Flying V and Moderne, was part of the rare and fabled 'Korina Trio'

Gibson Firebird

After the demise of the 'Korina Trio' in 1962, Ted McCarty still felt there was something to be gained from radical designs. Drafting in Ray Dietrich, a car designer, they came up with the reverse-body Firebird in 1963. As well as its futuristic shape, the Firebird embodied another first for Gibson – a through-neck with a new, distinctive headstock. New also, were the mini-humbuckers and banjo-style tuners that stuck straight out from the back of the headstock. There were four models, each with its own unique characteristics: the Firebird I was the only model to feature one pickup, the III had a simple vibrato, the V had trapezoid fret markers and the VII had three pickups, an ebony board and a first-fret position marker.

Firebird users are few and far between, although Brian Jones of The Rolling Stones was often seen with his model VII and Clapton played a Firebird I on Cream's farewell concert, offering Gibson much of the publicity it needed, and ensuring the Firebird's relative success. By 1965, the management had shifted at Gibson, Ted McCarty was on his way and attempts were made to standardise production. To this end, the non-reverse Firebird was introduced, with limited success. The model was discontinued in 1969.

Johnny Winter is perhaps the only bluesman who has used Firebirds over a significant length of time, his Firebird V providing the perfect stage for his inimitable brand of Texas slide. Today, it is the reverse-body models that are the most desired – just over 2,500 Firebird IIIs left Kalamazoo between 1963 and 1965, and only 303 Firebird VIIs

With its small humbucking pickups and slender mahogany body, the Firebird produced sharper tones than most Gibson electrics

Dobro/National

Despite the fact these guitars first appeared in the late 1920s, most people associate resonators with Mark Knopfler and the cover of Dire Straits' multi-million-selling *Brothers In Arms*. From a distance they appear simply as silver-plated acoustic guitars, yet the resonator concept represented a fundamental shift in guitar design; in some ways, they can be seen as bridging the gap between conventional acoustic guitars and electric instruments.

As bands grew during the 20s and 30s, John Dopyera, a Czech immigrant living in Los Angeles, recognised players' needs for greater volume in order to cut through. Rather than rely on the guitar's body for volume, he employed spun aluminium speaker-style cones to amplify the sound via the bridge, or 'biscuit', which sits directly on top of the cone. The result is a loud, metallic rasp which, when compared to an ordinary acoustic, sounds slightly harsh and unrefined. Yet that sound is so wonderfully evocative – whether it's coming from Mark Knopfler's fingerpicked 'Romeo And Juliet', or Hubert Sumlin's bluesy slide in 'I Can't Be Satisfied'.

The history of both Dobro and National is somewhat clouded, as the Dopyera Brothers were instrumental in both organisations, engaging in a number of buyouts, takeovers and law suits. Yet whatever the company history, resonator guitars quickly found their way into the hands of early bluesmen. Some opted for Hawaiian models (square neck, usually played like a lap steel), and others for the Spanish style (round neck, played like an ordinary guitar). Tuned to an open chord, and used with a slide, you are immediately greeted with that soulful tone straight from the heart of the Mississippi Delta. Tampa Red's output from the mid-1930s is a fine example of this style of playing, influencing Muddy Waters, Little Walter, Elmore James and BB King – all of whom covered his material.

Today, resonator guitars are highly desired, with both National and Dobro still producing a wide range of models. The original guitars are naturally the most valuable; their virtually bomb-proof construction means that even 1920s guitars remain in playable condition.

Today's National Delphi: its forefathers created the blues tones of the 1930s